General Assembly
Official Records
Sixty-seventh Session
Supplement No. 38

Report of the Committee on the Elimination of Discrimination against Women

**Forty-ninth session
(11-29 July 2011)**

**Fiftieth session
(3-21 October 2011)**

**Fifty-first session
(13 February-2 March 2012)**

United Nations • New York, 2012

Note

Symbols of United Nations documents are composed of capital letters combined with figures. Mention of such a symbol indicates a reference to a United Nations document.

The designations employed and the presentation of the material in this document do not imply the expression of any opinion whatsoever on the part of the Secretariat of the United Nations concerning the legal status of any country, territory, city or area or of its authorities, or concerning the delimitation of its frontiers or boundaries.

ISSN 0255-0970

Contents

Annexes

Annexes

Letter of transmittal

2 April 2012

I have the honour to refer to article 21 of the Convention on the Elimination of All Forms of Discrimination against Women, according to which the Committee on the Elimination of Discrimination against Women, established pursuant to the Convention, "shall, through the Economic and Social Council, report annually to the General Assembly of the United Nations on its activities".

The Committee on the Elimination of Discrimination against Women held its forty-ninth session, from 11 to 29 July 2011, at United Nations Headquarters in New York. It held its fiftieth session, from 3 to 21 October 2011, and its fifty-first session, from 13 February to 2 March 2012, at the United Nations Office at Geneva. It adopted its reports on the sessions at the 996th meeting, on 29 July 2011, the 1018th meeting, on 21 October 2011, and the 1038th meeting, on 2 March 2012, respectively. These three reports of the Committee are herewith submitted to you for transmission to the General Assembly at its sixty-seventh session.

(*Signed*) Silvia **Pimentel**
Chair

His Excellency Mr. Ban Ki-moon
Secretary-General of the United Nations
New York

Part One
Report of the Committee on the Elimination of Discrimination against Women on its forty-ninth session

11-29 July 2011

Chapter I

Matters brought to the attention of the States parties to the Convention on the Elimination of All Forms of Discrimination against Women

Decisions

Decision 49/I

The Committee decided to lift the simultaneous distribution policy with respect to its documentation on an indefinite basis. (See annex I to part one of the present report.)

Decision 49/II

The Committee decided to hold a day of general discussion on the draft general recommendation on women in armed conflict and post-conflict situations on 18 July 2011.

Decision 49/III

The Committee decided to send letters to the Governments of Egypt and Tunisia on the rights of women in the democratization process. (See annex II to part one of the present report.)

Decision 49/IV

On 21 July 2011, the Committee decided to confirm its current practice of referring to comments received from States parties relating to concluding observations of the Committee without reproducing them in its report. Furthermore, the Committee decided to post comments formally transmitted by States parties relating to concluding observations on its session web pages (www2.ohchr.org/english/bodies/cedaw) upon the request of the State party concerned, as received and without translation, and to provide a reference to the web page in its report.

Decision 49/V

The Committee decided to have a note verbale sent to the Permanent Mission of Belarus to the United Nations Office at Geneva, in response to the note verbale from that Permanent Mission dated 23 May 2011, noting that the practice of the Committee in regard to recording comments received from States parties is to refer to them in its reports to the General Assembly, and also informing the Mission that the Committee had decided to post such formal comments, including those received from Belarus, on its session web pages upon the request of the State party concerned. (See annex III to part one of the present report.)

Decision 49/VI

The Committee confirmed the members of the pre-session working group for the fifty-second session, namely Barbara Bailey, Meriem Belmihoub-Zerdani, Soledad Murillo de la Vega, Zohra Rasekh and Dubravka Šimonović.

Decision 49/VII

On 29 July 2011, the Committee adopted by vote the following decision, which was proposed by Ms. Patricia Schulz:

Having considered thoroughly the adoption procedure of general recommendations Nos. 27 and 28, which followed the rules of procedure of the Committee (A/56/38, annex) and was duly reflected in the report of the Committee to the General Assembly on its 47th session (A/66/38, part two), the Committee decided that references to general recommendations in its concluding observations and other outputs of the Committee should be made in a consistent fashion and follow the same format, i.e., title followed by year without any reference, footnote or other mention.

Discussion

Prior to the adoption of the above decision, an amendment to the proposal by Ms. Schulz was put forward by Ismat Jahan. In accordance with rule 37 of the rules of procedure of the Committee, the amendment was voted upon prior to the vote on the proposal by Ms. Schulz. The proposed amendment by Ms. Jahan reads as follows: "The Committee decides that references to general recommendations in its concluding observations and other outputs of the Committee shall be made in a consistent fashion and follow the same format, i.e., title followed by year, symbol of the report of the General Assembly, part, chapter and relevant paragraphs."

Prior to the vote, Ms. Jahan explained that the above format was being followed when the Committee referred to recommendations made by other treaty bodies or the universal periodic report in its concluding observations. It was also stated that the above format would be consistent and transparent. Ms. Schulz also took the floor stating that her proposal followed the practice of the Committee relating to its general recommendations.

The amendment was rejected, with 7 Committee members voting in favour and 15 members voting against, and no abstentions. The members who voted in favour of the amendment were Violet Awori, Meriem Belmihoub-Zerdani, Naéla Gabr, Ismat Jahan, Pramila Patten, Zohra Rasekh and Xiaoqiao Zou. The members who voted against the amendment were Ayse Feride Acar, Nicole Ameline, Magalys Arocha Dominguez, Barbara Bailey, Olinda Bareiro-Bobadilla, Niklas Bruun, Ruth Halperin-Kaddari, Yoko Hayashi, Soledad Murillo de la Vega, Violeta Neubauer, Silvia Pimentel, Maria Helena Pires, Victoria Popescu, Patricia Schulz and Dubravka Šimonović.

Following the vote on the amendment, the original proposal by Ms. Schulz was voted upon by a roll call vote in accordance with the rules of procedure of the Committee (rules 31, 32, 34, 37 and 38), with 15 members of the Committee voting in favour of the proposal and 7 members voting against the proposal, and no abstentions. The members who voted in favour of the proposal were Ayse Feride Acar, Nicole Ameline, Magalys Arocha Dominguez, Barbara Bailey, Olinda Bareiro-Bobadilla, Niklas Bruun, Ruth Halperin-Kaddari, Yoko Hayashi, Soledad Murillo de la Vega, Violeta Neubauer, Silvia Pimentel, Maria Helena Pires, Victoria Popescu, Patricia Schulz and Dubravka Šimonović. The members who voted against the proposal were Violet Awori, Meriem Belmihoub-Zerdani, Naéla Gabr, Ismat Jahan, Pramila Patten, Zohra Rasekh and Xiaoqiao Zou.

Following the adoption of the proposal by Ms. Schulz, Ms. Gabr took the floor and indicated her intention to submit a dissenting opinion. Ms. Belmihoub-Zerdani supported Ms. Gabr. Ms. Gabr subsequently submitted a letter signed by her, Ms. Belmihoub-Zerdani and Ms. Jahan, which stated as follows:

"As general recommendations Nos. 27 and 28 were adopted differently from all other general recommendations following a separate vote on some paragraphs, it is important for the sake of transparency and objectivity to provide the reader with a clear recollection of facts by making reference to the proceedings in the relevant report as follows: general recommendation No. 28 (A/66/38, part two, chap. VII, paras. 23 to 27); and general recommendation No. 27 (A/66/38, part two, chap. VII, paras. 28 and 29).

"We want this statement to be fully reflected in all reports of the Committee and reserve our right to make reference to it in the future when necessary."

Decision 49/VIII

On 29 July 2011, the Committee decided to adopt the following statement with respect to the Working Group on Working Methods:

The Committee has constantly refined its working methods in order to fulfil its responsibilities in an effective manner. It has improved its reporting guidelines and its constructive dialogue with the States parties and has refined its concluding observations. The Committee's desire to strengthen and rationalize its working methods will be a long-term project. In addition, the Committee's desire to strengthen its working methods is now taking place within the broader context of the treaty body strengthening process. Faced with a challenging workload, the Committee will need to continue to strengthen its working methods, also taking into consideration the harmonization of the treaty body system. As such, it is proposed that the task force on working methods should be transformed into a standing working group.

Decision 49/IX

On 29 July 2011, the Committee decided to adopt the following statement on the list of issues:

In order to assist in the prioritization of issues for the constructive dialogue and to keep replies as concise as possible (in some cases replies consist of 100 pages or more), it is proposed that the list of issues contain no more than 20 questions. Each question should contain no more than three issues.

Questions for the list of issues should be the types of questions which require research and not the type of questions that can be asked during the constructive dialogue.

The transmittal note template for the States parties indicates a page limit of 25 pages for replies; it also indicates that States parties may attach a limited number of additional pages of statistical data only.

It is also proposed that the transmittal letter be modified to clearly state that information contained in the reply should not repeat information already provided in the report.

Chapter II
Organizational and other matters

A. States parties to the Convention and to the Optional Protocol

1.   On 29 July 2011, the closing date of the forty-ninth session of the Committee on the Elimination of Discrimination against Women, there were 187 States parties to the Convention on the Elimination of All Forms of Discrimination against Women,[1] which was adopted by the General Assembly in its resolution 34/180 and opened for signature, ratification and accession in New York on 1 March 1980. In accordance with its article 27, the Convention entered into force on 3 September 1981. In addition, 64 States parties had accepted the amendment to article 20, paragraph 1, of the Convention, concerning the Committee's meeting time. A total of 125 States parties to the Convention are currently required to accept the amendment in order to bring it into force, in accordance with its provisions.

2.   As at the same date, there were 102 States parties to the Optional Protocol to the Convention,[2] which was adopted by the General Assembly in its resolution 54/4 and opened for signature, ratification and accession in New York on 10 December 1999. In accordance with its article 16, the Optional Protocol entered into force on 22 December 2000.

3.   Updated information on the Convention, the amendment to the Convention and its Optional Protocol, including lists of States signatories and parties and the texts of declarations, reservations, objections and other relevant information, can be found on the website of the United Nations Treaty Collection (http://treaties.un.org), maintained by the Treaty Section of the Office of Legal Affairs, which discharges the depositary functions of the Secretary-General.

B. Opening of the session

4.   The Committee held its forty-ninth session at United Nations Headquarters in New York from 11 to 29 July 2011. The Committee held 20 plenary meetings and also held 11 meetings to discuss agenda items 5, 6, 7 and 8. A list of the documents before the Committee is contained in annex IV to part one of the present report.

5.   The session was opened by the Chair of the Committee, Silvia Pimentel, on 11 July 2011 at its 977th meeting. Ivan Šimonović, Assistant Secretary-General, Office of the United Nations High Commissioner for Human Rights, addressed the Committee at the opening of the session.

C. Adoption of the agenda

6.   The Committee adopted the provisional agenda (CEDAW/C/49/1) at its 976th meeting.

---

[1] United Nations, *Treaty Series*, vol. 1249, No. 20378.
[2] Ibid., vol. 2131, No. 20378.

D. Report of the pre-session working group

7.   The report of the pre-session working group (CEDAW/PSWG/2010/49), which met from 25 to 29 October 2010, was introduced by its Chair, Violeta Neubauer, at the 977th meeting.

E. Organization of work

8.   On 11 July 2011, Maria Helena Lopes de Jesus Pires assumed her duties and took the solemn declaration as provided for in rule 15 of the rules of procedure of the Committee.

9.   On 11 July 2011, the Committee held a closed meeting with representatives of specialized agencies and United Nations funds and programmes, as well as other intergovernmental organizations, during which country-specific information, as well as information on the efforts made by those bodies to support the implementation of the Convention, was provided.

10.   On 11 and 18 July 2011, the Committee held informal public meetings with representatives of non-governmental organizations who provided information about the implementation of the Convention in the States parties reporting to the Committee at its forty-ninth session. The Committee held a meeting with an international human rights institution on 18 July 2011.

F. Membership of the Committee

11.   All members of the Committee except Indira Jaising attended the forty-ninth session. Ms. Pires was absent for a period of three days. Ms. Pires informed the Chair orally and in writing of the reason for the absence. A list of members of the Committee, indicating the duration of their terms of office, is contained in annex V to part one of the present report.

12-28161

Chapter III

Report of the Chair on the activities undertaken between the forty-ninth and fiftieth sessions of the Committee

12.   At the 977th meeting, the Chair presented her report on the activities she had undertaken since the forty-eighth session of the Committee.

Chapter IV

Consideration of reports submitted by States parties under article 18 of the Convention

13.   At its forty-ninth session, the Committee considered the reports of eight States parties submitted under article 18 of the Convention: the combined fifth and sixth periodic reports of Costa Rica, the combined initial, second and third periodic reports of Djibouti, the combined sixth and seventh periodic reports of Ethiopia, the sixth periodic report of Italy, the combined fourth and fifth periodic reports of Nepal, the seventh periodic report of the Republic of Korea, the fourth periodic report of Singapore and the combined fifth and sixth periodic report of Zambia. Information on the status of submission and consideration of reports submitted by States parties under article 18 of the Convention can be obtained from the Treaty Body Database under "reporting status" at www.unhchr.ch/tbs/doc.nsf.

14.   The Committee prepared concluding observations on each of the reports considered. Those observations are available through the Official Document System of the United Nations (http://documents.un.org/) under the symbol numbers indicated below:

Costa Rica	(CEDAW/C/CRI/CO/5-6)
Djibouti	(CEDAW/C/DJI/CO/1-3)
Ethiopia	(CEDAW/C/ETH/CO/6-7)
Italy	(CEDAW/C/ITA/CO/6)
Nepal	(CEDAW/C/NPL/CO/4-5)
Republic of Korea	(CEDAW/C/KOR/CO/7)
Singapore	(CEDAW/C/SGP/CO/4)
Zambia	(CEDAW/C/ZMB/CO/5-6)

Following the forty-ninth session, observations on the Committee's concluding observations were submitted by the Republic of Korea and Singapore.

Follow-up procedures relating to concluding observations

15.   The Committee adopted the report of the Rapporteur on follow-up at its forty-ninth session, and considered the follow-up reports received from the following States parties:

Azerbaijan	(CEDAW/C/AZE/CO/4/Add.1)
Portugal	(CEDAW/C/PRT/CO/7/Add.1)
Iceland	(CEDAW/C/ICE/CO/6/Add.1)

The follow-up reports of the States parties and the Committee's replies are available on the Committee's web page hosted on the OHCHR website under "follow-up reports" at www2.ohchr.org/english/bodies/cedaw.

16.   The Committee also sent reminders to the following States parties whose follow-up reports were overdue: Armenia, Cameroon, Germany and Rwanda. The Committee postponed sending a reminder to Libya.

17.   The Committee additionally sent second reminders to the following States parties to which it had already written requesting overdue follow-up reports: Belgium, Ecuador, El Salvador, Madagascar, Mongolia and Uruguay.

Chapter V

Activities carried out under the Optional Protocol to the Convention on the Elimination of All Forms of Discrimination against Women

18. Article 12 of the Optional Protocol to the Convention provides that the Committee shall include in its annual report under article 21 of the Convention a summary of its activities under the Optional Protocol.

A. Action taken by the Committee in respect of issues arising from article 2 of the Optional Protocol

19. The Committee discussed activities under the Optional Protocol on 25 July 2011.

20. The Committee endorsed the report of the Working Group on Communications under the Optional Protocol on its nineteenth and twentieth sessions (see annex VI to part one of the present report).

21. The Committee took action on communications Nos. 17/2008 (*Alyne Da Silva Pimentel v. Brazil*), 20/2008 (*Violeta Komova v. Bulgaria*) and 23/2009 (*Inga Abramova v. Belarus*) and adopted views on those communications by consensus.

22. In addition, the Committee decided:

   (a) To discontinue its consideration of communication No. 21/2009;

   (b) To allocate additional time for the consideration of communications at its fiftieth session.

B. Follow-up to views of the Committee on individual communications

23. No action was undertaken by the Committee regarding this item during the forty-ninth session, as the Permanent Mission of the Philippines was not available for a follow-up meeting in relation to communication No. 18/2008 (*Karen Tayag Vertido v. the Philippines*).

24. The Committee did not have any follow-up information to the views of the Committee to consider at this session. For the report of the Committee under the Optional Protocol on follow-up to views of the Committee on individual communications, see annex VII to part one of the present report.

C. Action taken by the Committee in respect of issues arising from article 8 of the Optional Protocol

25. No action was taken by the Committee at the forty-ninth session.

Chapter VI
Ways and means of expediting the work of the Committee

26. During its forty-ninth session, the Committee considered agenda item 7, on ways and means of expediting the work of the Committee.

Action taken by the Committee under agenda item 7

Enhancing the Committee's working methods

27. The Committee decided to transform the task force on working methods into a working group. Discussions took place in the Working Group on Working Methods relating to the pre-session working group, the constructive dialogue and the role of the country rapporteur.

28. Furthermore, the Committee was briefed on strengthening of the treaty body system within the context of the inter-committee meeting and the meeting of chairpersons of human rights bodies. All relevant documents were distributed to the members and are available through the OHCHR website (http://www2.ohchr.org/english/bodies/icm-mc/).

Dates of future sessions of the Committee

29. In accordance with the calendar of conferences, the following dates were confirmed for the Committee's fiftieth session and related meetings:

(a) Twenty-first session of the Working Group on Communications under the Optional Protocol: 28 to 30 September 2011, Geneva;

(b) Fiftieth session: 3-21 October 2011, Geneva;

(c) Pre-session working group for the fifty-second session: 24-28 October 2011, Geneva.

Reports to be considered at future sessions of the Committee

30. The Committee confirmed that it will consider the reports of the following States parties at its fiftieth session:

Fiftieth session:

Chad
Côte d'Ivoire
Kuwait
Lesotho
Mauritius
Montenegro
Oman
Paraguay

Chapter VII
Implementation of article 21 of the Convention

31. During the forty-ninth session, the Committee considered agenda item 6, on the implementation of article 21 of the Convention.

Action taken by the Committee under agenda item 6

General recommendation on the legal protection of women in conflict and post-conflict situations

32. The Committee held a general discussion on 18 July 2011 on women in conflict and post-conflict situations as the first phase in the elaboration of a general recommendation on the subject. Nearly 300 people attended the discussion. The discussion was opened by the Chair of the Committee, Silvia Pimentel, followed by opening addresses by Ivan Šimonović, Assistant Secretary-General, Office of the High Commissioner for Human Rights, and Lakshmi Puri, Assistant Secretary-General for Intergovernmental Support and Strategic Partnerships, UN-Women. The general recommendation on the legal protection of women in conflict and post-conflict situations was introduced by Pramila Patten, a member of the Committee and Chair of the working group on women in conflict and post-conflict situations. Keynote speakers included Margot Wallström, Special Representative of the Secretary-General on Sexual Violence in Conflict; Radhika Coomaraswamy, Special Representative of the Secretary-General for Children and Armed Conflict; Rashida Manjoo, Special Rapporteur on violence against women, its causes and consequences; Juan Mendez, Special Rapporteur on torture and other cruel, inhuman or degrading treatment or punishment; and Jessica Neuwirth, Coordinator of the High-Level Panel on Remedies and Reparations for Victims of Sexual Violence in the Democratic Republic of the Congo. Oral statements were made by representatives of the Office of the United Nations High Commissioner for Refugees (UNHCR), UN-Women and 17 civil society organizations, including Amnesty International, International Women's Rights Action Watch, the International Disability Alliance, Widows for Peace through Democracy, the International Alliance of Women, the Global Alliance against Traffic in Women, Global Action, the Forum for Women, Law and Development and others.

General recommendation on the economic consequences of marriage and its dissolution

33. No action was taken by the Committee in plenary at the forty-ninth session on this issue. However, the working group met during the session and further elaborated the general recommendation during a two-day retreat following the session on 31 July and 1 August 2011.

Joint general recommendation on harmful practices

34. No action was taken by the Committee on this issue at the forty-ninth session.

General recommendation on access to justice

35. No action was taken by the Committee on this issue at the forty-ninth session.

Task force on gender equality in the context of displacement and statelessness

36.   No action was taken by the Committee in plenary at the forty-ninth session, however, the Working Group met during the session.

Informal meeting

37.   The Committee held an informal meeting on Sunday, 10 July 2011 to discuss the issue of references in general recommendations No. 27 (Older women and protection of their human rights) and No. 28 (The core obligations of States parties under article 2 of the Convention) as well as other matters.

Chapter VIII
Provisional agenda for the fiftieth session

38.   The Committee considered the draft provisional agenda for its fiftieth session at its 996th meeting, on 29 July 2011, and approved the following provisional agenda for that session:

1.   Opening of the session.

2.   Adoption of the agenda and organization of work.

3.   Report of the Chairperson on activities undertaken between the forty-ninth and fiftieth sessions of the Committee.

4.   Consideration of reports submitted by States parties under article 18 of the Convention on the Elimination of All Forms of Discrimination against Women.

5.   Follow-up to concluding observations of reports submitted by States parties under article 18 of the Convention on the Elimination of All Forms of Discrimination against Women.

6.   Implementation of articles 21 and 22 of the Convention on the Elimination of All Forms of Discrimination against Women.

7.   Ways and means of expediting the work of the Committee.

8.   Activities of the Committee under the Optional Protocol to the Convention on the Elimination of All Forms of Discrimination against Women.

9.   Provisional agenda for the fifty-first session of the Committee.

10.   Adoption of the report of the Committee on its fiftieth session.

12-28161

Chapter IX
Adoption of the report

39. The Committee considered the draft report on its forty-ninth session and addenda on 29 July 2011 and adopted it as orally revised during the discussion.

Annex I

Decision 49/1. Exchange of letters on the lifting of the simultaneous distribution policy

Letter dated 11 March 2011 from the Chair of the Committee to the Chief of the Central Planning and Coordination Service, Division of Conference Management, United Nations Office at Geneva

As Chair of the Committee on the Elimination of Discrimination against Women, and on behalf of the Bureau of the said Committee, I am writing to request your urgent assistance with respect to the simultaneous distribution policy mandated by General Assembly resolution 50/11 on multilingualism.

Unfortunately, the above policy has the effect of hampering the treaty-mandated work of the Committee, which requires documents submitted for translation to be made available to the Committee as soon as they are issued in the various working languages of the Committee, without having to wait for all language versions to be finalized. Such documents include the reports by the States parties, the list of issues and replies thereto, as well as the concluding observations for purposes of adoption during the session.

As such, I would request that the above policy be suspended indefinitely, which will enable the Committee to discharge its functions more effectively.

I look forward to your confirmation of the above.

(*Signed*) Silvia **Pimentel**
Chair

Letter dated 14 March 2011 from the Chief of the Central Planning and Coordination Service, Division of Conference Management, United Nations Office at Geneva, to the Chair of the Committee

Thank you for your letter dated 11 March, regarding the waiving of General Assembly resolution 50/11 on simultaneous distribution of documents in all official languages. I wish to inform you that we have consulted the Department for General Assembly and Conference Management on this matter as it is the first request of its kind. Upon consultation with that Department, I am glad to inform you that electronic fair copies of documents could be shared with the Committee secretariat as languages become available, while maintaining simultaneous distribution for archiving documents on the Official Document System (ODS) and hard copy distribution.

I hasten to add that submission compliance and forecasting are encouraged in order to allow the Central Planning and Coordination Service to improve timely processing and issuance of documents.

The Secretary-General, in his memorandum to all heads of departments, funds and programmes, dated 25 February 2011, stated: "I would hereby strongly request that all departments/offices failing to meet the 90 per cent benchmark (compliance with slot dates) make immediate and robust efforts to reach that target." The submission compliance for OHCHR for 2010 was 35 per cent. It is therefore clear that any further improvement in timely issuance depends on improving timely submission of documents and minimizing last-minute requests by author departments.

(*Signed*) Ala **Almoman**
Chief of the Central Planning and Coordination Service
Division of Conference Management, United Nations Office at Geneva

Annex II

Decision 49/III. Letters from the Chair of the Committee to the Governments of Egypt and Tunisia

Identical letters dated 31 March 2011 from the Chair of the Committee to the Prime Minister and the Minister for Foreign Affairs of Egypt

On behalf of the Committee on the Elimination of Discrimination against Women, I have the honour to refer to the recent political developments in Egypt and the opportunity provided by such developments to recognize the important role of women in the call for change by ensuring that women's rights are a top priority for the Government of Egypt.

The Committee notes with concern that constitutional, legislative and policy initiatives and reforms may be undertaken without the full participation of Egyptian women. The Committee wishes to highlight in this regard that women's full participation is essential not only for their empowerment, but for the advancement of society as a whole.

As a State party to the Convention on the Elimination of All Forms of Discrimination against Women, Egypt has undertaken legally binding obligations to give effect to all of the provisions of the Convention with a view towards eliminating discrimination against women in all its forms and manifestations and the promotion of equality between men and women. The Convention also calls upon States parties to ensure the development and advancement of women and recognizes that the full and complete development of a country requires the maximum participation of women on equal terms with men in all fields, including the formulation of government policy and institution-building.

The Committee notes that the concept of democracy is only truly realized when political decision-making is shared by women and men alike and incorporates a gender perspective. As such, in the light of the above, the Committee urges the Government of the Arab Republic of Egypt to:

1.   Enable women to fully participate in the process of democratization at all levels of decision-making;

2.   Ensure that the constitutional, legislative and policy initiatives and reforms integrate the principle of non-discrimination as provided for in article 2 of the Convention, and respect for and enhancement of women's rights;

3.   Ensure that the implementation of such initiatives and reforms integrate a gender perspective and conform fully to the provisions of the Convention; and

4.   Ensure that the national mechanism on the rights of women is provided with a comprehensive and clear mandate and adequate financial and human resources to effectively discharge its functions.

(*Signed*) Silvia **Pimentel**
Chair

Identical letters dated 31 March 2011 from the Chair of the Committee to the Prime Minister and the Minister for Foreign Affairs of Tunisia

[Original: French]

On behalf of the Committee on the Elimination of Discrimination against Women, I have the honour to refer to the recent political developments in Tunisia and the opportunity provided by such developments to recognize the important role of women in the call for change by ensuring that women's rights are a top priority for the Tunisian Government.

The Committee notes with concern that constitutional, legislative and policy initiatives and reforms may be undertaken without the full participation of Tunisian women. The Committee wishes to highlight in this regard that women's full participation is essential not only for their empowerment, but for the advancement of society as a whole.

As a State party to the Convention on the Elimination of All Forms of Discrimination against Women, Tunisia has undertaken legally binding obligations to implement all the provisions of the Convention with a view towards eliminating discrimination against women in all its forms and promoting equality between men and women. The Convention also calls upon States parties to ensure the development and advancement of women and recognizes that the full and complete development of a country requires the maximum participation of women on equal terms with men in all fields, including the formulation of government policy and institution-building.

The Committee notes that the concept of democracy is only truly realized when political decision-making is shared equally between women and men and incorporates a gender perspective. As such, in the light of the above, the Committee urges the Government of Tunisia to:

1.   Enable women to fully participate in the process of democratization at all levels of decision-making;

2.   Ensure that constitutional, legislative and policy initiatives and reforms incorporate the principle of non-discrimination, as provided for in article 2 of the Convention, and respect for and enhancement of women's rights;

3.   Ensure that the implementation of such initiatives and reforms incorporates a gender perspective and conforms fully to the provisions of the Convention; and

4.   Ensure that the national mechanism on the rights of women is provided with a comprehensive and clear mandate and adequate financial and human resources to effectively discharge its functions.

Annex III

Decision 49/V. Exchange of notes verbales between the Permanent Mission of Belarus to the United Nations Office at Geneva and the Secretariat regarding comments to concluding observations of the Committee on the Elimination of Discrimination against Women

Note verbale dated 23 May 2011 from the Permanent Mission of Belarus addressed to the Secretariat

[For the text of the note verbale from the Permanent Mission of Belarus, please refer to the web page of the forty-eighth session of the Committee at www2.ohchr.org/english/bodies/cedaw/docs/Noteverbale23_05_11_Belarus_CEDAW48.pdf.]

Note verbale dated 22 July 2011 from the Secretariat addressed to the Permanent Mission of Belarus

The Secretariat of the United Nations (Office of the High Commissioner for Human Rights) presents its compliments to the Permanent Mission of Belarus to the United Nations Office and other international organizations at Geneva and has the honour to refer to the Permanent Mission's note verbale (reference No. 606) dated 23 May 2011.

The Secretariat has duly transmitted the note verbale to the Committee on the Elimination of Discrimination against Women. As previously noted, the practice of the Committee in regard to recording comments received from States parties is to refer to them in its reports to the General Assembly. Furthermore, the Committee decided to post all such formal comments, including those received from Belarus, on its session web pages which can be accessed on the website of the Office of the High Commissioner for Human Rights.

Annex IV

Documents before the Committee at its forty-ninth session

Document number	Title or description
CEDAW/C/49/1	Provisional agenda and annotations
CEDAW/C/48/2	Report of the Secretary-General on the status of submission of reports by States parties under article 18 of the Convention
CEDAW/C/49/3	Note by the Secretary-General on reports provided by the specialized agencies of the United Nations system on the implementation of the Convention in areas falling within the scope of their activities
CEDAW/C/49/3/Add.2	Note by the Secretary-General containing the report of the United Nations Educational, Scientific and Cultural Organization
CEDAW/C/49/3/Add.4	Note by the Secretary-General containing the report of the International Labour Organization
CEDAW/C/49/4	Note by the Secretariat on ways and means of expediting the work of the Committee

Reports of States parties

CEDAW/C/CRI/5-6	Combined fifth and sixth periodic reports of Costa Rica
CEDAW/C/DJI/1-3	Combined initial, second and third periodic reports of Djibouti
CEDAW/C/ETH/6-7	Combined sixth and seventh periodic reports of Ethiopia
CEDAW/C/ITA/6	Sixth periodic report of Italy
CEDAW/C/NPL/4-5	Combined fourth and fifth periodic reports of Nepal
CEDAW/C/KOR/7	Seventh periodic report of the Republic of Korea
CEDAW/C/SGP/4	Fourth periodic report of Singapore
CEDAW/C/ZMB/5-6	Combined fifth and sixth periodic reports of Zambia

Annex V

Membership of the Committee on the Elimination of Discrimination against Women as at 1 April 2012

Name of member	Country of nationality	Term of office expires on 31 December
Ayse Feride Acar	Turkey	2014
Nicole Ameline	France	2012
Olinda Bareiro-Bobadilla	Paraguay	2014
Magalys Arocha Dominguez	Cuba	2012
Violet Tsisiga Awori	Kenya	2012
Barbara Evelyn Bailey	Jamaica	2012
Meriem Belmihoub-Zerdani	Algeria	2014
Niklas Bruun	Finland	2012
Naéla Mohamed Gabr	Egypt	2014
Ruth Halperin-Kaddari	Israel	2014
Yoko Hayashi	Japan	2014
Ismat Jahan	Bangladesh	2014
Indira Jaising	India	2012
Soledad Murillo de la Vega	Spain	2012
Violeta Neubauer	Slovenia	2014
Pramila Patten	Mauritius	2014
Silvia Pimentel	Brazil	2012
Maria Helena Lopes de Jesus Pires	Timor-Leste	2014
Victoria Popescu	Romania	2012
Zohra Rasekh	Afghanistan	2012
Patricia Schulz	Switzerland	2014
Dubravka Šimonović	Croatia	2014
Xiaoqiao Zou	China	2012

Annex VI

Report of the Working Group on Communications under the Optional Protocol to the Convention on the Elimination of All Forms of Discrimination against Women on its nineteenth and twentieth sessions

1.   The Working Group on Communications under the Optional Protocol to the Convention on the Elimination of All Forms of Discrimination against Women held its nineteenth session from 7 to 10 February 2011 and its twentieth session from 6 to 8 July 2011. Dubravka Šimonović was elected as Chair and Yoko Hayashi as Vice-Chair of the Working Group. All members attended the sessions. Ms. Hayashi was absent on the last day of the nineteenth session of the Working Group.

2.   At the beginning of each session, the Working Group adopted its agenda as set out in the appendices to the present report.

3.   At its nineteenth session, the Working Group reviewed the update on new correspondence received by the Secretariat since its last session, presented in a format with more detailed information, and concluded that a paragraph should be added providing statistics on the correspondence, including the number of pieces of correspondence with regard to States not parties. At its twentieth session, the Working Group had before it a table of correspondence received or processed between 15 December 2010 and 6 May 2011 as well as a table dividing that correspondence into four categories, as requested by the Working Group at its nineteenth session.

4.   At both sessions, the Working Group reviewed the status of pending registered communications and had a discussion on each one of them.

5.   At its nineteenth session, the Working Group discussed a draft recommendation in relation to the admissibility and merits of communication No. 17/2008 and two draft recommendations on admissibility in relation to communications Nos. 21/2009 and 22/2009. It also had a discussion on communication No. 20/2008.

6.   At its twentieth session, the Working Group discussed a draft recommendation in relation to the admissibility and merits of communication No. 22/2008 and a draft recommendation in relation to the admissibility of communication No. 27/2010. It also had a preliminary discussion on communication No. 28/2010 and deliberated on whether or not the consideration of communications Nos. 21/2009 and 25/2010 should be discontinued.

7.   At its nineteenth session, the Working Group discussed correspondence in relation to a request for interim measures from a Ugandan woman fearing female genital mutilation if returned to Uganda from Denmark. At its twentieth session, the Working Group continued its discussion on that case and also discussed correspondence in relation to a new case concerning the Philippines. It further considered a request from the Government of Canada under the Canadian Access to Information Act asking the Committee's consent to release two diplomatic notes received from the Committee in relation to communication No. 25/2010.

8.   The Working Group discussed working methods, including the number of sessions per year, requests from States parties to deal with admissibility and merits separately (so-called "split requests"), the practice of other treaty bodies to declare communications partly admissible/inadmissible, and outreach activities.

9.   The Working Group took note of four articles on the Committee's views in relation to communication No. 18/2008 (*Karen Tayag Vertido v. the Philippines*).

Actions taken

10.   At its nineteenth session, the Working Group decided:

(a)   That its twentieth session would be held from 6 to 8 July 2011 in New York and its twenty-first session would be held from 28 to 30 September 2011 in Geneva;

(b)   To register two new cases against Bulgaria as communications No. 31/2011 (Ms. Šimonović was appointed as case rapporteur) and No. 32/2011 (Niklas Bruun was appointed as case rapporteur);

(c)   To appoint Olinda Bareiro-Bobadilla as case rapporteur for communication No. 22/2008 and exceptionally as co-rapporteur for communication No. 17/2008 together with Magalys Arocha Dominguez;

(d)   To appoint Mr. Bruun as case rapporteur for communication No. 28/2010;

(e)   To seek information on the exact subject matter of the author's case before the European Court of Human Rights in communication No. 27/2010;

(f)   To issue interim measures in communication No. 29/2011, requesting the Spanish authorities not expel the author of the communication while her complaint is under consideration by the Committee. A vote was held in relation to the request for interim measures; 4 members voted in favour and 1 member abstained;

(g)   To grant the request submitted by Canada to consider separately the admissibility and merits of communications Nos. 25/2010 and 26/2010 and to discuss these communications at the twenty-first session of the Working Group in September 2011;

(h)   To send a final letter to the Government of Georgia in relation to communication No. 24/2009 informing it that the Committee would proceed with the examination of the admissibility and merits of the communication, if no response was received by 31 May 2011. A meeting with the Permanent Mission should be organized during the twentieth session, if the State party fails to cooperate with the Committee;

(i)   To prepare communications Nos. 20/2008, 22/2009, 23/2009 and 27/2010 for the twentieth session of the Working Group in July 2011 and, if appropriate, forward them to the Committee at its forty-ninth session;

(j)   To prepare draft recommendations in relation to the merits of communication No. 19/2008 and the admissibility of communication No. 26/2010 and, to the extent possible, draft recommendations in relation to the admissibility and merits of communication No. 24/2010 and the admissibility of communication No. 25/2010 for the twenty-first session of the Working Group;

(k)   To have a preliminary discussion on communication No. 28/2010 at the twentieth session and on communications Nos. 30/2011 and 31/2011 at the twenty-first session of the Working Group;

(l)   To request the Secretariat to prepare a paper on the practice of declaring inadmissible communications where the matter has been examined or is being examined under another procedure of international investigation or settlement;

(m)   To include follow-up to the Committee's views as a standing item in the agenda of the Working Group;

(n)   To request the Secretariat to explore the possibility of organizing briefings for non-governmental organizations on the Optional Protocol procedures;

(o)   To create a reference file of all articles in relation to the Optional Protocol work which have been distributed to date;

(p)   To request the Secretariat to explore the possibility of improving the Internet page on the Optional Protocol to make it more user-friendly and to include follow-up information together with the views;

(q)   To maintain the current distribution of the 10 days per year available to the Working Group, i.e., it will meet three times per year and will work between sessions in order to avoid possible delays for the October sessions.

11.   At its twentieth session, the Working Group decided:

(a)   To adopt recommendations in relation to the admissibility and merits of communications Nos. 17/2008, 20/2008 and 23/2008;

(b)   To register two new cases, one against Denmark as communication No. 33/2011 (Mr. Bruun was appointed as case rapporteur) and one against the Philippines as communication No. 34/2011 (Ms. Šimonović was appointed as case rapporteur);

(c)   To issue interim measures in the case (registered as communication No. 33/2011) concerning a Ugandan woman fearing female genital mutilation if returned to Uganda from Denmark, requesting the Danish authorities not to expel the author of the communication while her complaint is under consideration by the Committee. On 13 July 2011, the Committee transmitted the communication to the State party, at the same time requesting it not to expel the author to Uganda while her communication was under consideration by the Committee. On 19 July 2011, the State party replied that, pursuant to the Committee's request, the expulsion order against the author had been suspended until further notice;

(d)   To discontinue its consideration of communication No. 21/2009 and to include a paragraph in its annual report stating that, owing to the clear intention expressed by the author to pursue her case before the European Court of Human Rights, the Committee had decided to discontinue its consideration of the case;

(e)   To review the Committee's rules of procedure in relation to discontinuances at the twenty-first session of the Working Group;

(f)   To schedule a follow-up meeting with the Permanent Mission of the Philippines to the United Nations in New York during the third week of the Committee's forty-ninth session to remind the State party of its obligation to compensate the author of communication No. 18/2008, even in the absence of an explicit article in the Convention providing for compensation, and to prepare a note verbale strongly reiterating this obligation by reference to the Committee's jurisprudence in *A.T. v. Hungary*, its general recommendation No. 28 and treaty bodies' common practice;

(g)   To send a reply to the Government of Canada concerning its request to release two diplomatic notes in relation to communication No. 25/2010, informing the State party that in accordance with rule 74, paragraph 7, of the Committee's rules of procedure, nothing prevents the State party from making public any submission or information bearing on the proceedings. A draft letter should be sent to the case rapporteur, Pramila Patten;

(h)   To send a reminder to the Government of Canada asking it to send its observations on the merits of communication No. 19/2008;

(i)   To send a formal reminder to counsel asking him to submit comments on the State party's observations dated 6 December 2010 concerning the admissibility of communication No. 25/2010;

(j)   To request the Government of Turkey in relation to communication No. 28/2010 to provide translations of the decisions of the Labour Court and the Court of Appeal dated 14 September 2007 and 2 April 2009, respectively;

(k)   To request a copy of the decision of the European Court of Human Rights which declared inadmissible the application submitted by the author of communication No. 27/2010 and to prepare a new draft recommendation in relation to the admissibility of that communication based on article 4, paragraph 2 (c), of the Optional Protocol for the twenty-first session of the Working Group;

(l)   In addition to the cases identified in paragraphs 10 (j) and 11 (k) above, to prepare draft recommendations in relation to the admissibility and merits of communication No. 22/2009 and in relation to the admissibility of communications Nos. 26/2010 and 29/2011 for the twenty-first session of the Working Group in September 2011 and, if appropriate, forward them to the Committee at its fiftieth session;

(m)   That the Secretariat should send any new correspondence concerning registered cases to the respective case rapporteur;

(n)   To postpone its discussion of working methods, including follow-up on views and duplication of international procedures ("forum shopping"), to its twenty-first session;

(o)   To have a discussion during its twenty-first session on the possibility of declaring communications partly admissible/inadmissible, taking into account the jurisprudence of other treaty bodies;

(p)   To take a fresh look at its twenty-first session at the current distribution of the 10 days per year available to the Working Group;

(q)   To restructure the table of correspondence received or processed in the note by the Secretariat so that it reflects which correspondence concerns prima facie inadmissible complaints and/or has been disposed of by means of a standard letter and which correspondence concerns potentially admissible and/or more complicated cases;

(r)   To suggest to the plenary that additional time be allocated to the consideration of communications at the forty-ninth and fiftieth sessions of the Committee.

12.   The Working Group submitted the following issues for the Committee's consideration and decision:

(a)   Recommendations relating to the admissibility and merits of communications Nos. 17/2008 (*Pimentel v. Brazil*), 20/2008 (*Komova v. Bulgaria*) and 23/2009 (*Abramova v. Belarus*);

(b)   A recommendation to discontinue the consideration of communication No. 21/2009 and to include a paragraph in the Committee's annual report stating that, owing to the clear intention expressed by the author to pursue her case before the European Court of Human Rights, the Committee had decided to discontinue its consideration of the case;

(c)   Schedule a follow-up meeting with the Permanent Mission of the Philippines to the United Nations in New York during the third week of the Committee's forty-ninth session to remind the State party of its obligation to compensate the author of communication No. 18/2008, even in the absence of an explicit article in the Convention providing for compensation;

(d)   Send a note verbale to the Government of the Philippines strongly recalling its obligation to compensate the author of communication No. 18/2008 by reference to the Committee's jurisprudence in *A.T. v. Hungary*, its general recommendation No. 28 and the common practice of treaty bodies;

(e)   Send a reply to the Government of Canada concerning its request to release two diplomatic notes in relation to communication No. 25/2010, informing the State party that nothing prevents it from making public any submission or information bearing on the proceedings;

(f)   Request the Secretariat to explore the possibility of organizing briefings for non-governmental organizations on the Optional Protocol procedures;

(g)   Request the Secretariat to explore the possibility of improving the Internet page on the Optional Protocol to make it more user-friendly and to include follow-up information together with the views;

(h)   Allocate additional time to the consideration of communications at the forty-ninth and fiftieth sessions of the Committee.

Appendix I

Agenda of the nineteenth session of the Working Group

1. Adoption of the agenda and organization of work.

2. Review of steps and activities undertaken since the last session.

3. Discussion of two summaries prepared by the Secretariat for registration.

4. Discussion on case No. 22/2009.

5. Discussion on case No. 17/2008.

6. Discussion on case No. 21/2009.

7. Update of communications Nos. 20/2008, 23/2009, 24/2009, 25/2010, 26/2010, 27/2010, 28/2010 and 29/2011.

8. Discussion on working methods and outreach activities for the Optional Protocol.

9. Adoption of the report of the Working Group on its nineteenth session.

12-28161

Appendix II

Agenda of the twentieth session of the Working Group

1. Adoption of the agenda and organization of work.

2. Review of steps and activities undertaken since the last session.

3. Discussion on registration of new communications.

4. Discussion on cases ready for adoption:

    CEDAW/C/WGCOP/20/DR/17/2008 (draft on admissibility and merits)

    CEDAW/C/WGCOP/20/DR/20/2008 (draft on admissibility and merits)

    CEDAW/C/WGCOP/20/DR/22/2008 (draft on admissibility and merits)

    CEDAW/C/WGCOP/20/DR/23/2009 (draft on admissibility and merits)

    CEDAW/C/WGCOP/20/DR/27/2010 (draft inadmissibility decision)

5. Cases for discontinuance.

6. Update of communications.

7. Preliminary discussion on case No. 28/2010.

8. Update on follow-up on views.

9. Discussion on working methods, including follow-up on views, "forum shopping", number of sessions per year and others.

10. Adoption of the report of the Working Group on its twentieth session.

Annex VII

Report of the Committee under the Optional Protocol on follow-up to views of the Committee on individual communications

1.   Under article 7, paragraphs 4 and 5, of the Optional Protocol to the Convention on the Elimination of All Forms of Discrimination against Women (see General Assembly resolution 54/4, annex), States parties are obliged to give due consideration to the views and recommendations of the Committee, if any, and to submit follow-up information within six months. Further information may be sought from the State party, including in its subsequent reports. Rule 73 of the Committee's rules of procedure (A/56/38, annex I) relates to the procedure for follow-up to the views of the Committee, in particular the designation and functions of the rapporteur or working group on follow-up. Rule 74(11) states that information on follow-up, including the decisions of the Committee on follow-up, shall not be confidential unless otherwise decided by the Committee. For previous follow-up information, please refer to past annual reports of the Committee on the Elimination of Discrimination against Women.

2.   As per the established practice, in situations where the Committee does not make a final decision on the nature of a State party's response, it states that the dialogue is "ongoing". Where a satisfactory response has been received, the case is considered closed, as the Committee has already done in the case of *A.T. v. Hungary*, communication No. 2/2003, and of *S.A. v. Hungary*, communication No. 4/2004.

3.   A summary of all information on follow-up to the Committee's views received from the authors and States parties after the adoption of the previous annual report of the Committee, up to the end of the fifty-first session, is provided in the table below. For further information concerning the Committee's follow-up activities on individual communications, see the reports of the Working Group on Communications included in annex VI to part one, annex IV to part two and annex III to part three of the present report.

State party	The Philippines
Case	18/2010, Karen Vertido
Views adopted on	16 July 2010
Violations found	The State party has failed to fulfil its obligations and has thereby violated the rights of the author under article 2 (c) and (f) and article 5 (a) read in conjunction with article 1 of the Convention, and general recommendation No. 19 of the Committee.
Remedy	*Concerning the author of the communication* Provide appropriate compensation commensurate with the gravity of the violations of her rights.

General

Take effective measures to ensure that court proceedings involving rape allegations are pursued without undue delay.

Ensure that all legal procedures in cases involving crimes of rape and other sexual offences are impartial and fair, and not affected by prejudices or stereotypical gender notions. To achieve this, a wide range of measures are needed, targeted at the legal system, to improve the judicial handling of rape cases, as well as training and education to change discriminatory attitudes towards women. Concrete measures include:

(i)   Review of the definition of rape in the legislation so as to place the lack of consent at its centre;

(ii)   Removal of any requirement in the legislation that sexual assault be committed by force or violence, and any requirement of proof of penetration, and minimization of secondary victimization of the complainant/survivor in proceedings by enacting a definition of sexual assault that either:

a. Requires the existence of "unequivocal and voluntary agreement" and requiring proof by the accused of steps taken to ascertain whether the complainant/survivor was consenting; or

b. Requires that the act take place in "coercive circumstances" and includes a broad range of coercive circumstances; [h]

(iii) Appropriate and regular training on the Convention on the Elimination of All Forms of Discrimination against Women, its Optional Protocol and its general recommendations, in particular general recommendation No. 19, for judges, lawyers and law enforcement personnel;

(iv) Appropriate training for judges, lawyers, law enforcement officers and medical personnel in understanding crimes of rape and other sexual offences in a gender-sensitive manner so as to avoid re-victimization of women having reported rape cases and to ensure that personal mores and values do not affect decision-making.

Due date for State party's reply	19 April 2011
Date of reply	13 April 2011
State party's reply	On 13 April 2011, the State party informed the Committee that it welcomes the views and that it has given careful consideration to the recommendations contained therein.

As to the Committee's recommendation to grant the author appropriate compensation, the State party reiterates that the author has failed to exhaust available domestic remedies. The State party's legislation provides multiple avenues through which the author may claim compensation, without prejudice to statute of limitations. The author could have pursued a civil case for compensation, independently of the criminal prosecution of the offence; an acquittal does not automatically preclude a judgment against the accused in the civil aspect of the case where acquittal is based on reasonable doubts. Since the acquittal in the present case was based on insufficient evidence, the author could have pursued the civil aspect and thus could have been granted compensation.

Moreover, the State party submits that Philippine laws permit a victim of, inter alia, a violent crime (including rape) to seek compensation before the Board of Claims pursuant to Republic Act No. 7309, "Compensation". This action, however, should have been initiated within six months after the injury suffered, but the author has failed to avail herself of these proceedings.

The State party further notes that the Committee's recommendation for the provision of adequate compensation is not based on an explicit obligation of the State party under the Convention.

The State party adds that its judiciary is independent and has exclusive jurisdiction in determining guilt or innocence of an accused. As to the Committee's recommendations concerning the effective measures to ensure that court proceedings involving rape are pursued without undue delay, the State party submits that it advocates and supports the protection and promotion of human rights, including those in judicial proceedings, and is undertaking measures to ensure that the Speedy Trial Act of 1998 is fully and effectively implemented.

As to the measures to ensure that legal procedures, inter alia, in rape cases are fair and impartial and not affected by prejudices or stereotypical gender notions, the State party explains that the laws and jurisprudence of the Philippines show that an essential element for the commission of the crime of rape is the lack of consent on the part of the victim. Nonetheless, the State party has *motu propio* launched a campaign, through the Philippine Commission on Women, to review and fine-tune the current penal definition of the crime of rape to make sure that lack of consent is considered as the essential element of the crime. The proposed bill to amend the Anti-Rape Law of 1997 is also envisaged to include principles of the appreciation of evidence, specify the conduct and procedure of a trial, etc.

In addition, since 2006 the Philippine Judicial Academy has been conducting training for judges, lawyers and court clerks to get them acquainted with the Convention and to promote gender sensitization in courts.

Moreover, in 2008 five training sessions entitled "Workshop for members of the Committee on Decorum and Investigation" were carried out involving over 200 judges, lawyers and other clerks. A discussion on gender equality and the Convention on the Elimination of All Forms of Discrimination against Women was also attended by justices of the Court of Appeals.

As to the further measures to assist and protect victims of rape, the State party explains that since the passing of the 1998 Rape Victim Assistance and Protection Act with the aim of providing necessary assistance and protection for rape victims, in coordination with relevant State agencies and non-governmental organizations, rape crisis centres were established in every province and the city to assist and protect rape victims in the litigation of their cases and in their recovery.

Notably, the Rape Victim Assistance and Protection Act prescribes that in prosecutions of rape, evidence of a complainant's past sexual conduct, opinion thereof or his/her reputation shall not be admitted, unless and only to the extent that the court finds that such evidence is material and relevant to the case.

Finally, the State party submits that the full text of the Committee's views and recommendations is available through the Philippine Gender and Development Portal of the Philippine Commission on Women.

Author's comments   On 17 June 2011, the author provided her comments to the State party's observations, and contended that the Committee's views had not been implemented and she had not been compensated for the discrimination suffered. According to her, the State party does not recognize her as a victim of violation of the Convention.

As to the State party's submission that the author should have sought compensation under civil action, the author emphasizes that her claim of discrimination was not against the accused who raped her, but against the State party which violated both her rights and its obligations under the Convention in the rape case she had filed. The author's objective in her rape case was not to seek compensation, but to seek justice. While she understands that compensation is a part of the criminal proceedings, it would have only determined if the accused was found guilty. If she had decided to pursue a pecuniary or non-pecuniary claim after the perpetrator's acquittal, she would have litigated her claim for many years more while trying to prove with great difficulty that she has a right to compensation despite the acquittal.

As to the Republic Act No. 7309, the author indicates that only victims of violent crime, including rape, may be compensated under this law. Since the responsible judge in her case concluded that no crime of rape was committed, this remedy is inapplicable to her situation. In addition, if the author were qualified to be compensated under that Act, the maximum amount that she would have been entitled to would be around US$ 230.

As to the State party's observation on the independence of the judiciary, the author recalls that the judiciary is part of the State. According to her, the State party has failed in its obligation under the Convention to ensure the existence of competent national tribunals which do not engage in discrimination against women.

Further, as to the training of judges, the author believes that the existing training programmes are inadequate and have failed to produce positive results, particularly in the manner judges handle sexual violence cases. The author qualifies discrimination against women in court as systematic.

Moreover, as to the Speedy Trial Act of 1998, the author maintains that her own case demonstrates that such cases last for many years before they are concluded in court.

Finally, with respect to the Rape Victim Assistance and Protection Act of 1998, the author submits that according to an exhaustive study, as of April 2001 no rape crisis centre had been established under this Act, due to lack of corresponding financial means. In 2011, i.e., more than 12 years after the enactment of the Act, the State party has only started the initial phase of implementing the Act by setting up two pilot rape crisis centres.

Further action taken	In accordance with the Committee's request, the Secretariat has tried, without success, to organize a meeting with representatives of the State party's Permanent Mission to the United Nations Office at Geneva, in 2011 and 2012.
Committee's decision	Follow-up dialogue ongoing.

Part Two
Report of the Committee on the Elimination of Discrimination against Women on its fiftieth session

3-21 October 2011

Chapter I

Matters brought to the attention of the States parties to the Convention on the Elimination of All Forms of Discrimination against Women

Decisions

Decision 50/I

On 17 October 2011, the Committee adopted the following decision with respect to enhancing the constructive dialogue with the State parties:

Based on its previous practice, the Committee shall establish task forces for the constructive dialogue with States parties, as a pilot project, during the fifty-first and fifty-second sessions. An evaluation of the impact of this task force approach shall be conducted by the Committee during its fifty-second session. Country rapporteurs shall take a leading role in coordinating work in task forces.

The members of the Committee shall express their options for joining the task forces of the fifty-first and fifty-second sessions, in consultation with the country rapporteurs, during the sessions preceding each of those sessions. The membership of the task forces will be finalized in an informal meeting of the Committee as a whole, at the end of each of the preceding session, and will be reflected in the Chair's intersessional letter.

Membership of a task force should not exceed 14 experts. In order to facilitate coordination of task force members so that all main areas of concern are covered in an appropriate manner, the country rapporteurs should organize task force meetings no later than the day preceding the dialogue. Country rapporteurs should also brief the Committee as a whole on the main concerns relating to the country reports during the afternoon meeting of the day before the dialogue.

The members of a task force may have at most two interventions during the constructive dialogue. Time allocation for interventions should take into account the number of interventions per article of the Convention, as follows: 6 minutes for a single speaker and 3 minutes per speaker when there are two or more speakers for the same article.

Furthermore, any Committee member may ask follow-up questions limited to 2 minutes each, if time allows.

The Committee shall strive for better time management during the constructive dialogue. Committee members should prioritize their interventions, limit the number of issues raised and focus on matters most relevant for the country under consideration. During the constructive dialogue experts should not repeat questions asked previously, neither should they resume questions contained in the List of Issues unless these have not been properly and satisfactorily answered. To facilitate better time management, it is proposed that the Committee covers sections I and II of the Convention until 1 p.m. and sections III and IV until 5 p.m.

The Chair will continue to coordinate with the head of delegation with respect to time management, providing guidance and reminders when appropriate throughout the dialogue, including reminders to provide precise and brief answers.

Likewise, the Chair will advise the delegation to avoid reading out lists of statistics and supply them in writing instead.

It is the prerogative of the Chair to move the questions relating to articles 15 and 16 (part IV), when appropriate, in consultation with the country rapporteur, so that they are considered together with the questions in part I. This decision should be announced in the beginning of the dialogue.

Decision 50/II

On 17 October 2011, the Committee adopted the following decision with respect to strengthening the role of the country rapporteur:

Country rapporteurs shall have a more prominent role in providing guidance to experts in the preparation of and during the constructive dialogues, in the drafting and adoption of concluding observations, as well as in handling comments from States parties in response to concluding observations.

Country rapporteurs shall conduct informal consultations with experts in order to ensure full coverage of main areas of concern in the country and to prevent any overlap. Country rapporteurs should also brief the Committee as a whole on the main concerns relating to the country reports, during the afternoon meeting of the day before the dialogue.

It is proposed that better coordination be ensured between the country rapporteurs, the pre-session working groups and the Secretariat. The country rapporteurs shall endeavour to provide inputs to the pre-session working group with respect to the countries concerned even if they are not members of the pre-session working group. The Secretariat shall also endeavour to assign the same staff member who worked on a particular country during the pre-session working group to the same country for purposes of the constructive dialogue.

The country rapporteurs shall also provide the country briefing notes as early as possible to the Secretariat, no later than one week prior to the session. In this regard, the Secretariat shall make available all information and inputs from the United Nations country team and from other sources as early as possible. The same applies to the output of the pre-session working group and the background notes prepared by the Secretariat. It is further noted that all such materials are posted on the Committee's extranet as soon as they are made available to the Secretariat.

Country rapporteurs' notes shall not repeat information contained in the background notes prepared by the Secretariat. These notes shall also include succinct information about the sociopolitical context of the country and shall focus on main areas of concern (not necessarily on an article-by-article basis) as well as on suggestions of recommendations.

The Secretariat, in consultation with the Working Group on Working Methods, shall develop a template for the country rapporteurs' briefing notes.

Decision 50/III

On 18 October 2011, the Committee decided to establish an open-ended task force on inquiries, which would establish its terms of reference in accordance with the rules of procedure of the Committee regarding inquiries.

Decision 50/IV

On 18 October 2011, the Committee decided to establish a joint working group with the Human Rights Committee.

Decision 50/V

On 19 October 2011, the Committee decided to adopt a statement on the anniversaries of the adoptions of the 1951 Convention relating to the Status of Refugees and the 1961 Convention on the Reduction of Statelessness. (See annex I to part two of the present report.)

Decision 50/VI

On 19 October 2011, the Committee decided to adopt a statement on rural women. (See annex II to part two of the present report.)

Decision 50/VII

The Committee decided to establish a working group on rural women for purposes of establishing a general recommendation in this regard. The Committee also decided that any work on a general recommendation would take place intersessionally until decided otherwise by the Committee.

Decision 50/VIII

The Committee decided to transform the existing task force into the working group on gender equality in the context of asylum, statelessness and natural disasters for purposes of establishing a general recommendation in this regard. The Committee also decided that any work on a general recommendation would take place intersessionally until decided otherwise by the Committee.

Decision 50/IX

The Committee decided to appoint Dubravka Šimonović as focal point for the United Nations Entity for Gender Equality and the Empowerment of Women (UN-Women) and Zohra Rasekh as alternate focal point.

Decision 50/X

The Committee decided to appoint Zohra Rasekh as focal point for HIV and gender equality.

Chapter II
Organizational and other matters

A. States parties to the Convention and to the Optional Protocol

1. On 21 October 2011, the closing date of the fiftieth session of the Committee on the Elimination of Discrimination against Women, there were 187 States parties to the Convention on the Elimination of All Forms of Discrimination against Women, which was adopted by the General Assembly in its resolution 34/180 and opened for signature, ratification and accession in New York on 1 March 1980. In accordance with its article 27, the Convention entered into force on 3 September 1981. In addition, 64 States parties had accepted the amendment to article 20, paragraph 1, of the Convention, concerning the Committee's meeting time. A total of 125 States parties to the Convention are currently required to accept the amendment in order to bring it into force, in accordance with its provisions.

2. As at the same date, there were 103 States parties to the Optional Protocol to the Convention, which was adopted by the General Assembly in its resolution 54/4 and opened for signature in New York on 10 December 1999. In accordance with its article 16, the Optional Protocol entered into force on 22 December 2000.

3. Updated information on the status of the Convention, the amendment to the Convention and its Optional Protocol, including lists of States signatories and parties as well as the texts of declarations, reservations, objections and other relevant information, can be found on the website of the United Nations Treaty Collection (http://treaties.un.org), maintained by the Treaty Section of the Office of Legal Affairs, which discharges the depositary functions of the Secretary-General.

B. Opening of the session

4. The Committee held its fiftieth session at the United Nations Office at Geneva from 3 to 21 October 2011. The Committee held 19 plenary meetings and also held 11 meetings to discuss agenda items 5, 6, 7 and 8. A list of the documents before the Committee is contained in annex III to part two of the present report.

5. The session was opened by the Chair of the Committee, Silvia Pimentel on 3 October 2011. The High Commissioner for Human Rights, Navi Pillay, addressed the Committee at the opening of the session.

C. Adoption of the agenda

6. The Committee adopted the provisional agenda (CEDAW/C/50/1) at its 996th meeting.

D. Report of the pre-session working group

7. The report of the pre-session working group (CEDAW/PSWG/50/1), which met from 7 to 11 February 2011, was introduced by Nicole Ameline at the 997th meeting.

E. Organization of work

8.   On 3 October 2011, the Committee held a closed meeting with representatives of specialized agencies and United Nations funds and programmes, as well as other intergovernmental organizations, during which those bodies provided country-specific information as well as information on the efforts they had made to support the implementation of the Convention.

9.   On 3 and 10 October 2011, the Committee held informal public meetings with representatives of non-governmental organizations who provided information about the implementation of the Convention in the countries whose Governments were reporting to the Committee at its fiftieth session.

F. Membership of the Committee

10.   All members except Indira Jaising attended the fiftieth session. Ruth Halperin-Kaddari and Xiaoqiao Zou were not able to attend the last three days of the session. A list of members of the Committee, indicating the duration of their terms of office, is contained in annex V to part one of the present report.

12-28161

Chapter III

Report of the Chair on the activities undertaken between the forty-ninth and fiftieth sessions of the Committee

11.   At the 997th meeting, the Chair presented a report on the activities she had undertaken since the forty-ninth session of the Committee.

Chapter IV

Consideration of reports submitted by States parties under article 18 of the Convention

12.   At its fiftieth session, the Committee considered the reports of eight States parties submitted under article 18 of the Convention: the combined initial, second, third and fourth periodic reports of Chad; the combined initial, second and third periodic reports of Côte d'Ivoire; the combined third and fourth periodic reports of Kuwait; the combined initial, second, third and fourth periodic reports of Lesotho; the combined sixth and seventh periodic reports of Mauritius; the initial report of Montenegro; the initial report of Oman; and the sixth periodic report of Paraguay. Information on the status of submission and consideration of reports submitted by States parties under article 18 of the Convention can be obtained from the Treaty Body Database under "reporting status" at www.unhchr.ch/tbs/doc.nsf.

13.   The Committee prepared concluding observations on each of the reports considered. Those observations are available from the Official Document System of the United Nations (http://documents.un.org/) under the symbol numbers indicated below:

Chad	(CEDAW/C/TCD/CO/1-4)
Côte d'Ivoire	(CEDAW/C/CIV/CO/1-3)
Kuwait	(CEDAW/C/KWT/CO/3-4)
Lesotho	(CEDAW/C/LSO/CO/1-4)
Mauritius	(CEDAW/C/MUS/CO/6-7)
Montenegro	(CEDAW/C/MNE/CO/1)
Oman	(CEDAW/C/OMN/CO/1)
Paraguay	(CEDAW/C/PRY/CO/6)

Following the fiftieth session, observations on concluding observations of the Committee were submitted by Mauritius and Montenegro.

Follow-up procedures relating to concluding observations

14.   The Committee adopted the report of the rapporteur on follow-up at its fiftieth session, and considered the follow-up reports and additional information received from the following States parties:

Denmark	(CEDAW/C/DEN/CO/7/Add.1)
Germany	(CEDAW/C/DEU/CO/6/Add.1)
Japan	(CEDAW/C/JPN/CO/6/Add.1)
Kyrgyzstan	(CEDAW/C/KGZ/CO/3/Add.1)
Myanmar	(CEDAW/C/MMR/CO/3/Add.3)

The follow-up reports and additional information received from the States parties and the Committee's replies are available on the Committee's web page hosted on the OHCHR website under "follow-up reports" at http://www2.ohchr.org/english/bodies/cedaw.

15.   The Committee also sent reminders to the following States parties whose follow-up reports were overdue: Bhutan, Guinea-Bissau, Lao People's Democratic Republic, Liberia, Spain, Switzerland and Timor-Leste.

16.   The Committee also sent letters to Nigeria and the United Republic of Tanzania to schedule meetings with representatives of those States parties, who had not submitted their follow-up report despite two reminders sent by the Committee. As the Committee did not receive any reply, the meetings will be rescheduled for the fifty-first session.

17.   While additional information from Canada was not due until October 2012, Canada sent a letter stating that it would provide additional information in the next periodic report due on 2014. As a result, the Committee decided to close the follow-up procedure on Canada.

Assessment of follow-up procedure to concluding observations

18.   The rapporteur on follow-up presented an assessment of the follow-up procedure since the forty-first session, in accordance with the decision taken at that session.

19.   Given the relatively short time of two years during which the follow-up procedure has been implemented, the information contained in the reports submitted suggests that the follow-up procedure is achieving its stated goal of acting as a tool of implementation of the Convention and more specifically the recommendations set out in selected concluding observations. This procedure is therefore proving to be an effective reporting procedure under the article 18 of the Convention that enables the Committee to monitor progress achieved between reporting cycles.

20.   It is clear, however, that over time the workload will increase incrementally and that Committee members and the Secretariat will need to allocate adequate time to this agenda item.

21.   The following recommendations were agreed to by the Committee:

        (a)   The follow-up procedure on the implementation of concluding observations should continue under article 18 of the Convention;

        (b)   The two-year mandate of the rapporteur on follow-up and the alternate should be retained, and all Committee members should participate in follow-up assessment on a rotating basis;

        (c)   The methodology for follow-up should be retained;

        (d)   A country-specific follow-up approach is needed for States parties in conflict or in a post-conflict situation who do not report under the follow-up procedure; that approach should include appropriate technical assistance;

        (e)   In addition to the separate agenda item on follow-up, which should continue, increased time should be allocated during the Committee's session and a specific staff person should be assigned to the follow-up procedure to ensure timely support both during and between sessions;

        (f)   The next evaluation of the process should be carried out and tabled at the October 2013 session.

Appointment of rapporteur on follow-up and alternate rapporteur

22.   Ms. Šimonović decided to withdraw from the function of rapporteur on follow-up to concluding observations, although the end of her mandate was on 31 December 2012. The Committee decided to appoint Ms. Bailey (previous alternate rapporteur) as the new rapporteur on follow-up and Ms. Hayashi as alternate rapporteur for a period of two years, until 31 December 2013, in accordance with the decision of the Committee, at its forty-fifth session, to provide a mandate of two years to the rapporteur and his or her alternate.

Chapter V

Activities carried out under the Optional Protocol to the Convention on the Elimination of All Forms of Discrimination against Women

23. Article 12 of the Optional Protocol to the Convention on the Elimination of All Forms of Discrimination against Women provides that the Committee shall include in its annual report a summary of its activities carried out under the Optional Protocol.

A. Action taken by the Committee in respect of issues arising from article 2 of the Optional Protocol

24. The Committee discussed activities under the Optional Protocol on 17 and 18 October 2011.

25. The Committee endorsed the report of the Working Group on Communications under the Optional Protocol on its twenty-first session (see annex IV to part two of the present report).

26. The Committee took action on communications Nos. 22/2009 (*C.P. v. Peru*), 26/2010 (*Herrera Riveira v. Canada*) and 27/2010 (*Z.M. v. Italy*) and adopted one view and two inadmissibility decisions on those communications by consensus.

27. In addition, the Committee took the following decisions:

    (a) To maintain the current format of three Committee sessions, including one session in New York, serviced by the Petitions Unit;

    (b) To improve the Committee's website with a view to reflecting all cases adopted by the Committee, including discontinuance decisions;

    (c) To include information on the Optional Protocol in the Committee's extranet page, to ensure that members have access to updated information on all registered cases;

    (d) To develop a methodology with regard to follow-up over the year to come.

B. Follow-up to views of the Committee on individual communications

28. The Committee decided to appoint the following rapporteurs on follow-up: case No. 17/2008 (*Pimentel v. Brazil*): Ms. Bareiro-Bobadilla and Ms. Arocha; case No. 20/2008 (*V. K. v. Bulgaria*): Ms. Šimonović and Ms. Popescu; case No. 23/2009 (*Abramova v. Belarus*): Ms. Hayashi, Ms. Neubauer and Ms. Schulz.

29. No specific follow-up action could be undertaken this session in relation to communication No. 18/2008 (*Karen Tayag Vertido v. the Philippines*), as the Permanent Mission of the Philippines had not responded to the Committee's request for a follow-up meeting, transmitted early in the session. For the report of the Committee under the Optional Protocol on follow-up to views of the Committee on individual communications, see annex VII to part one of the present report).

C. Action taken by the Committee in respect of issues arising from article 8 of the Optional Protocol

30.   A request for an inquiry was received and registered by the Secretariat (request for inquiry No. 2011/3), and members of the Committee were appointed to undertake a preliminary consideration of the information received, in accordance with rule 82 of the rules of procedure of the Committee. The Committee also examined information relating to request for. inquiry No. 2011/2 and decided to request additional information on the matter. The Committee further examined information relating to request for inquiry No. 2011/1 and decided to pursue the matter in accordance with rule 84 of the rules of procedure, but did not decide at this session to establish an inquiry. The Committee was also briefed on the status of inquiry No. 2010/1.

12-28161

Chapter VI
Ways and means of expediting the work of the Committee

31.   During its fiftieth session, the Committee considered agenda item 7, on ways and means of expediting the work of the Committee.

Action taken by the Committee under agenda item 7

Enhancing the Committee's working methods

32.   The Working Group on Working Methods met during the session and presented to the Committee a draft decision relating to the establishment of task forces for the consideration of States parties' reports and a draft decision relating to the enhancement of the role of the country rapporteur, which were adopted by the Committee. The Committee adopted the drafts as decision 50/I (one member abstained) and 50/II (by consensus) (see chap. I of part two of the present report).

33.   Furthermore, the Committee was briefed on the strengthening of the treaty body system within the context of the Inter-Committee Meeting and the Meeting of the Chairpersons by Navi Pillay, the High Commissioner for Human Rights, and Ibrahim Salama, Director of the Human Rights Treaties Division. In addition, Wan-Hea Lee of the Groups in Focus Section of the Human Rights Treaties Division of OHCHR gave a briefing on the list of issues prior to reporting, which was followed by a discussion in plenary on its relevance for the work of the Committee. Comments from the Committee referred to the specificity of the Convention with respect to other human rights instruments, compatibility of the procedure with States' reporting obligations as contained in the Convention, and concerns regarding alternative sources of information for an effective, constructive dialogue in the absence of a report.

34.   The Committee also met with the Human Rights Committee to discuss working methods, specifically, the list of issues prior to reporting and follow-up to concluding observations, and decided to establish a joint working group with the Human Rights Committee for future cooperation.

Dates of future sessions of the Committee

35.   In accordance with the calendar of conferences, the following dates and places were confirmed for the Committee's fifty-first and fifty-second sessions and related meetings:

(a)   Twenty-second session of the Working Group on Communications under the Optional Protocol: 7-10 February 2012, Geneva;

(b)   Fifty-first session: 13 February-2 March 2012, Geneva;

(c)   Pre-session working group for the fifty-third session: 5-9 March 2012, Geneva;

(d)   Twenty-third session of the Working Group on Communications under the Optional Protocol: 4-6 July 2011, New York;

(e)   Fifty-second session: 9-27 July 2012, New York;

(f)   Pre-session working group for the fifty-fourth session: 30 July-3 August 2012, New York.

Reports to be considered at future sessions of the Committee

36.   The Committee confirmed that it would consider the reports of the States parties listed below at its fifty-first and fifty-second sessions.

Fifty-first session

Algeria
Brazil
Congo
Grenada
Jordan
Norway
Zimbabwe

Fifty-second session

Bahamas
Bulgaria
Guyana
Indonesia
Jamaica
Mexico
New Zealand
Samoa

Chapter VII
Implementation of article 21 of the Convention

37. During the fiftieth session, the Committee considered agenda item 6, on the implementation of article 21 of the Convention.

Action taken by the Committee under agenda item 6

General recommendation on the economic consequences of marriage and its dissolution

38. The working group met during the session and the Committee was presented with the finalized draft version of the general recommendation for a first reading.

General recommendation on the human rights of women in armed conflict and post-conflict situations

39. The working group met during the session but no discussions took place in plenary. The working group also met with the working group on gender equality in the context of displacement and statelessness to ensure that the general recommendation on the human rights of women in armed conflict and post-conflict situations and the future general recommendation on gender equality in the context of displacement and statelessness would be complementary and would not overlap.

Joint general recommendation on harmful practices

40. The working group met during the session and also held a joint meeting with the working group of the Committee on the Rights of the Child to review an annotated outline of the general recommendation. There was no discussion in plenary on this issue.

General recommendation on access to justice

41. A draft concept note was circulated to the Committee at this session. The working group also met.

Working group on gender equality in the context of asylum, statelessness and natural disasters

42. A meeting took place between the task force on gender equality in the context of asylum, statelessness and natural disasters and UNHCR on the elaboration of a statement on gender equality in the context of displacement and statelessness relating to the anniversaries of the adoption of the 1951 Convention relating to the Status of Refugees and the 1961 Convention on the Reduction of Statelessness. The statement was adopted during the fiftieth session. The Committee also decided to transform the task force into a working group for the purpose of establishing a general recommendation in this regard. The Committee additionally decided that any work on a general recommendation would take place between sessions until decided otherwise by the Committee.

Working group on rural women

43.   The Committee decided to establish a working group on rural women for the purpose of establishing a general recommendation in this regard. The Committee also decided that any work on a general recommendation would take place between sessions until decided otherwise by the Committee.

Chapter VIII
Provisional agenda for the fifty-first session

44. The Committee considered the draft provisional agenda for its fifty-first session on 21 October 2011 and approved the following provisional agenda for that session:

1. Opening of the session.

2. Adoption of the agenda and organization of work.

3. Report of the Chair on activities undertaken between the fiftieth and fifty-first sessions of the Committee.

4. Consideration of reports submitted by States parties under article 18 of the Convention on the Elimination of All Forms of Discrimination against Women.

5. Follow-up to concluding observations of reports submitted by States parties under article 18 of the Convention on the Elimination of All Forms of Discrimination against Women.

6. Implementation of articles 21 and 22 of the Convention on the Elimination of All Forms of Discrimination against Women.

7. Ways and means of expediting the work of the Committee.

8. Activities of the Committee under the Optional Protocol to the Convention on the Elimination of All Forms of Discrimination against Women.

9. Provisional agenda for the fifty-second session of the Committee.

10. Adoption of the report of the Committee on its fifty-first session.

Chapter IX
Adoption of the report

45.   The Committee considered the draft report on its fiftieth session on 21 October 2011 and adopted it as orally revised during the discussion.

Annex I

Decision 50/V. Statement of the Committee on the Elimination of Discrimination against Women on the anniversaries of the adoption of the 1951 Convention relating to the Status of Refugees and the 1961 Convention on the Reduction of Statelessness

Adopted on 19 October 2011 during the fiftieth session

A call for gender equality for refugees and stateless persons

Together with the 1951 Convention relating to the Status of Refugees (1951 Refugee Convention) as amended by its 1967 Protocol and the 1961 Convention on the Reduction of Statelessness, the 1979 Convention on the Elimination of All Forms of Discrimination against Women provides universal standards for the treatment of refugee and stateless women and girls. These instruments are complementary and their full implementation is essential to achieving gender equality.

On the occasion of the sixtieth anniversary of the 1951 Refugee Convention and the fiftieth anniversary of the 1961 Convention on the Reduction of Statelessness, the Committee on the Elimination of Discrimination against Women requests all State parties to the Convention on the Elimination of All Forms of Discrimination against Women to reaffirm their commitment to adhering to their international obligations by ensuring that their laws, policies and practices do not discriminate against refugee and stateless women and girls.

The Convention on the Elimination of All Forms of Discrimination against Women promotes gender equality and sets out measures for the advancement of all women without distinction on the basis of their nationality/citizenship or other legal status, such as refugee, migration or marital status. Gender discrimination and inequality against women and girls can be the result of and intensified by forced displacement and statelessness. Situations of forced displacement and statelessness often impact women and girls differently and include sexual and gender-based violence and discrimination against women.

The Convention on the Elimination of All Forms of Discrimination against Women applies at every stage of the displacement cycle. Asylum claims made by women may be based on any of the grounds in the 1951 Convention, but they may also be based on gender-related forms of persecution. The Committee calls upon States to recognize gender-related forms of persecution and to interpret the "membership of a particular social group" ground of the 1951 Convention to apply to women.[3] Gender-sensitive registration, reception, interview and adjudication processes also need to be in place to ensure women's equal access to asylum.

The Committee likewise calls upon States to implement safeguards against sexual and gender-related violence against women and girls in refugee settings and

---

[3] See also conclusion No. 39 (XXXVI) refugee women and international protection of the Executive Committee of the Programme of the United Nations High Commissioner for Refugees, 18 October 1985, para. (k).

to provide remedies for such violations, to empower women by ensuring their equal participation in refugee leadership positions, including within peacebuilding processes in accordance with the Convention on the Elimination of All Forms of Discrimination against Women and Security Council resolution 1325 (2000). It also calls upon States to guarantee women equal rights and access to health services, education, food, shelter, security, free movement and opportunities in their search for justice and durable solutions.[4]

In relation to statelessness, the Convention on the Elimination of All Forms of Discrimination against Women is a significant tool in international efforts to prevent and reduce statelessness arising from discrimination against women with regard to nationality rights. The Convention requires full protection of women's equality in nationality matters. It provides that States shall ensure that marriage does not automatically change the nationality of the wife, render her stateless or force upon her the nationality of the husband. States parties are also obliged to grant women equal rights with men to transfer nationality to their foreign spouse as well as their children (article 9 of the Convention). The Committee welcomes the legislative changes made by a number of States parties to change discriminatory nationality laws. Problems persist, however, in approximately 30 countries worldwide.

Notwithstanding the progress made so far, much remains to be done to achieve gender equality, not least within the contexts of displacement and statelessness. The Committee recognizes that the protection risks faced by women and girls, in particular the scourges of gender-based violence, sexual violence, domestic violence and human trafficking, continue to be of paramount concern. The Committee calls upon States to remain seized of these issues as a matter of priority and to further strengthen the protection of women and girls.

The Committee also encourages States that have not yet done so to accede to the 1951 Refugee Convention and its 1967 Protocol, the 1954 Convention on the Status of Stateless Persons, the 1961 Convention on the Reduction of Statelessness and the Convention on the Elimination of All Forms of Discrimination against Women and its Optional Protocol, to withdraw any continuing reservations to these instruments and to establish national legal frameworks on asylum and statelessness that respect gender equality principles.

---

[4] See also conclusion No. 105 (LVII) on women and girls at risk of the Executive Committee of the Programme of the United Nations High Commissioner for Refugees, 6 October 2006.

Annex II

Decision 50/VI. General statement of the Committee on the Elimination of Discrimination against Women on rural women

Adopted on 19 October 2011 during the fiftieth session

The situation of rural women has been at the forefront of the United Nations agenda for many years, including in the General Assembly, the Economic and Social Council, the Commission on the Status of Women and the Committee on the Elimination of Discrimination against Women and in various United Nations agencies. It is also linked to the effective and full implementation of the Millennium Development Goals.

In light of the upcoming fifty-sixth session of the Commission on the Status of Women with the priority theme "The empowerment of rural women and their role in poverty and hunger eradication, development and current challenges", the Committee on the Elimination of Discrimination against Women takes the opportunity to make a general statement on rural women.

Normative framework

The Committee is mandated, inter alia, to specifically address the rights, needs and concerns of rural women. Article 14 of the Convention on the Elimination of All Forms of Discrimination against Women states that States parties shall take into account the particular problems faced by rural women and the significant roles which rural women play in the economic survival of their families, including their work in the non-monetized sectors of the economy, and shall take all appropriate measures to ensure the application of the provisions of the Convention to women in rural areas. States parties shall take all appropriate measures to eliminate discrimination against women in rural areas in order to ensure, on a basis of equality of men and women, that they participate in and benefit from rural development.

In its general recommendation No. 16 on unpaid women workers in rural and urban family enterprises, the Committee recommends that States parties take the necessary steps to guarantee payment, social security and social benefits for women who work without such benefits in enterprises owned by a family member.

The Committee's general recommendation No. 19 on violence against women states that rural women are at risk of gender-based violence due to traditional attitudes regarding the subordinate role of women that persist in many rural communities. Girls from rural communities are at special risk of violence and sexual exploitation when they leave the rural community to seek employment in towns.

Empowerment

The Committee stresses that despite efforts undertaken to encourage the overall empowerment of rural women, there are still many issues that need to be addressed as women, and in particular rural women, face discrimination in all spheres of life.

Education and literacy

Two thirds of the roughly 1 billion illiterates in the world are women and girls. Worldwide, girls from rural areas are particularly disadvantaged, with the lowest levels of literacy and education. Available figures show that only 5 per cent of services such as education programmes and training courses have been addressed to rural women. Notably, literacy programmes for girls and women are not easily accessible to more remote rural communities. Distance to schools, fear of sexual assault on the way to school or at school and early pregnancy, together with often heavy household responsibilities, discourage or prevent girls from seizing education opportunities.

Health

Rural women are particularly disadvantaged with respect to their access to health-care services. Maternal mortality continues to be strikingly high in rural areas — 640 deaths per 100,000 live births compared with 447 in urban areas. In every region of the world, the presence of skilled birth attendants and medical personnel is lower in rural than in urban areas. Obstetric fistula, a condition that often develops during obstructed labour, is more prevalent among rural women as a result of malnutrition, pregnancy at a young age and difficult working conditions. In addition, access to overall health care of the girl child, who is usually neglected owing to prevailing patriarchal attitudes in many traditional rural settings that give preference to boys, is often very poor.

Access to resources and opportunities

Rural women have less access to resources, training and skill development opportunities owing to illiteracy, the prevalence of negative stereotypes and their overall socioeconomic status. This limits their effective participation in the community. As a consequence, in some regions, they are further suffering from discrimination in relation to their right to land ownership and transfer of property. Reduction of rural poverty depends on improving the access of women to decent work and income-generating opportunities, particularly by ensuring their access to productive assets including land, credit and technology and developing their skills and human capital. Reducing hunger and malnutrition depends on real and equal access to and control over productive resources for both men and women in rural areas. Investing in women farmers and closing the gender gap in agricultural productivity would reduce the number of undernourished people by 12 to 17 per cent. That translates into 100 to 150 million fewer people living in hunger. Despite the recognized role of women in combating food insecurity and poverty, and the importance of women's access to sustainable energy, water, sanitation, education, nutrition and health to the overall development of a country, necessary funding has not matched policy commitments. Of the $18.4 billion spent on agricultural aid between 2002 and 2008, donors reported that just 5.6 per cent included a gender focus.

In some countries, only 10 per cent of credit allowances are extended to women, especially rural women, mainly because national legislation and customary law do not allow them to share land ownership/property rights along with their husbands or male members of their families, or because female heads of household are excluded from land entitlement schemes and consequently cannot provide the collateral required by lending institutions.

Rural women also have very limited employment opportunities in general, and when they seek off-farm employment they tend to be engaged in less skilled and less financially rewarding jobs. Microfinance credits to rural women and micro-, small- and medium-sized enterprises for women's self-employment also need to be promoted.

Agriculture, hunger and poverty

Rural women are key partners in economic and social development. According to comparable data, women comprise an average of 43 per cent of the agricultural labour force of developing countries. In fact, in many countries they are the backbone of local and national food security and a critical force in reducing poverty, malnutrition and hunger and in promoting development. Yet, when it comes to investments and policies, women's contribution to food security and agricultural production is often unpaid, largely invisible, frequently ignored and generally undersupported. Rural women's needs for agricultural technologies, labour-saving agricultural equipment and modern means of communication have to be addressed, as do the valuing and counting of their non-monetized contribution to the economic survival of families and to national development.

Agriculture is inextricably linked to poverty eradication, especially in developing countries. The main challenges to agricultural productivity include negative impacts of climate change, natural disasters and human-made disasters, e.g., internal conflicts which disproportionately affect rural women. In addition, the lease and sale of large tracts of land to other States or to large private companies, as well as the patenting of seeds, tend to reduce the chances that women will be able to provide adequate food to themselves and their families. Rural women have a central role in combating these negative effects and must therefore be involved in all relevant programmes aimed at addressing these challenges, including preservation of the natural environment and preserving the quality of food.

Conflict situations

Rural women often bear the major burden in armed conflict and post-conflict situations. They are subjected to violations of basic human rights such as the rights to life, safety and freedom of movement, as well as their rights to productivity, livelihood, access to food and health care. In addition, they face forced displacement, sexual violence and loss of family members and children. Despite some attention given to women in conflict, the situation of rural women in times of armed conflict and post-conflict is often ignored.

Violence, trafficking, sexual exploitation and forced labour

Violence against women, trafficking in women, sexual exploitation and forced labour are often linked to poverty and lack of opportunities in rural areas. Such root causes of violence and trafficking should be addressed through targeted legislative and policy measures. Rural women in conflict and post-conflict situations are affected disproportionally. The special situation of these women needs focused attention.

Participatory development

The Committee recognizes the importance of rural women's participation as critical agents of development such as agricultural producers, entrepreneurs and managers of natural resources. It emphasizes the crucial role that rural women play with respect to enhancing agricultural and rural development, improving food security and eradicating poverty. The Committee also underscores the right of rural women and women's organizations to participate in decision-making processes which impact on their lives including through representation in parliaments, bodies of local governance and the entities entrusted with negotiating and implementing sales and leasing of national land to foreign States and/or private companies.

Recommendations

The Committee calls upon all Member States and the United Nations, its programmes, funds and agencies to contribute towards the achievement of gender equality in rural areas and stresses the importance and the need for coordinated action on a broad scale in partnership with civil society, as appropriate, to increase rural women's overall empowerment and their contributions to agricultural productivity and eradication of poverty and hunger, in particular by:

(a) Incorporating gender-sensitive perspectives when designing and implementing rural development strategies, policies and programmes, including the objective of gender equality as an overarching goal of such strategies, policies and programmes, and adopting and implementing temporary special measures in favour of rural women;

(b) Renouncing policies that might limit the ability of rural women to provide for adequate food for themselves, their families and communities, such as purchasing seeds with genetic use restriction technology patents, which produce sterile plants so that farmers must buy seeds each planting season instead of using seeds produced by the plants themselves;

(c) Involving rural women in all aspects of planning, implementation and evaluation of all policies and programmes impacting their lives;

(d) Enhancing the representation of rural women in parliaments and executive bodies, as well as in bodies of national and local governance, including those responsible for planning, negotiating, selling or leasing national land;

(e) Ensuring rural women's equal access to basic social services such as housing, education, health care, including maternal, sexual and reproductive health-care services, childcare facilities and means of transportation;

(f) Providing social safety networks to help rural women in developing countries face the impact of economic restructuring and food price volatility;

(g) Promoting full employment and decent work for rural women, including income-generating activities;

(h) Reducing rural women's labour time and work effort with infrastructure and technological innovation;

(i) Ensuring rural women's equal, easy and affordable access to productive resources, energy, water, land use and ownership and property, environmentally sound technologies, financing and microcredits, extension and agribusiness services, vocational and non-vocational training programmes and markets;

(j)   Integrally incorporating women's concerns and participation in the planning, implementation and monitoring of all development and environmental management programmes to ensure women's involvement, which is necessary for their benefit as well as for the achievement of sustainable development;

(k)   Adopting systematic measures to increase rural women's awareness of the scope of their rights and undertaking general awareness-raising campaigns to educate society about the roles, rights and status of rural women, including through government programmes, the media and civil society initiatives, as well as through traditional leaders, in order to combat traditions, stereotypes, customary laws and practices that discriminate against rural women;

(l)   Ensuring rural women's access to justice and the supporting institutional mechanisms necessary to fulfil their rights, so that rural women can realize their full potential in every respect;

(m) Developing strategies to address the special needs of older women, disabled women and indigenous women living in rural areas, who often suffer a severe lack of basic resources for subsistence, income security, access to health care, information on and enjoyment of their entitlements and rights.

Annex III

Documents before the Committee at its fiftieth session

Document number	Title or description
CEDAW/C/50/1	Provisional agenda and schedule of dialogues
CEDAW/C/2010/48/2	Report of the Secretary-General on the status of submission of reports by States parties under article 18 of the Convention (updated annually)
CEDAW/C/50/3	Report of the International Labour Organization
CEDAW/C/50/4	Report of the United Nations Educational, Scientific and Cultural Organization

Reports of States parties

Document number	Title or description
CEDAW/C/TCD/1-4	Combined initial to fourth periodic reports of Chad
CEDAW/C/CIV/1-3	Combined initial to third periodic reports of Côte d'Ivoire
CEDAW/C/KWT/3-4	Combined third and fourth periodic reports of Kuwait
CEDAW/C/LSO/1-4	Combined initial to fourth periodic reports of Lesotho
CEDAW/C/MUS/6-7	Combined sixth and seventh periodic reports of Mauritius
CEDAW/C/MNE/1	Initial report of Montenegro
CEDAW/C/OMN/1	Initial report of Oman
CEDAW/C/PAR/6 and Corr.1	Sixth periodic report of Paraguay

12-28161

Annex IV

Report of the Working Group on Communications under the Optional Protocol to the Convention on the Elimination of All Forms of Discrimination against Women on its twenty-first session

1. The Working Group on Communications under the Optional Protocol to the Convention on the Elimination of All Forms of Discrimination against Women held its twenty-first session from 28 to 30 September 2011. All members attended the session.

2. At the beginning of the session, the Working Group adopted its agenda as set out in the appendix to the present report.

3. At its twenty-first session, the Working Group reviewed the update on new correspondence received by the Secretariat since its last session. The Working Group had before it a table of correspondence received or processed between 7 May and 2 August 2011, as well as a table dividing that correspondence into five categories, as requested by the Working Group at its twentieth session.

4. During its session, the Working Group reviewed the status of pending registered communications and had a discussion on each one of them.

5. The Working Group discussed a draft recommendation in relation to the admissibility and merits of communication No. 22/2009, and three draft recommendations on admissibility in relation to communications Nos. 26/2010, 27/2010 and 29/2011. Owing to the unavailability of translation of draft recommendation 29/2011 (original in Spanish), the Working Group decided to postpone consideration of that case to its twenty-second session.

6. The Working Group also had a discussion on communication No. 19/2008 and engaged in a preliminary discussion on communication No. 30/2011.

7. The Working Group considered a request from the State party in communication No. 24/2009 for the Committee to "contribute to securing a friendly settlement" with the author.

8. The Working Group also discussed a request of the State party, in relation to communication No. 32/2011, that the Committee examine the admissibility of the case separately from its merits.

9. The Working Group discussed working methods, including the number of its sessions per year, servicing from the Secretariat and methods governing its intersessional work on communications, and the practice of other treaty bodies.

10. The Working Group discussed follow-up and the appointment of follow-up rapporteurs. Ms. Bareiro-Bobadilla provided a brief presentation on steps so far taken by the Brazilian authorities to publicize the Committee's recommendation No. 17/2008.

11. The Working Group took note of several publications referred to by the Secretariat relevant to its work on communications.

Actions taken

12.   At its twenty-first session, the Working Group decided:

(a)   To adopt a recommendation in relation to the admissibility and merits of communication No. 22/2009, and recommendations in relation to the admissibility of communications Nos. 26/2010 and 27/2010;

(b)   To send an ultimate reminder to counsel, in communication No. 25/2010, for his comments on the State party's observations on admissibility, with a one-month deadline;

(c)   To send the author a letter asking her to respond to specific issues raised in the State party's submission on the merits of communication No. 19/2008, within the deadline of 26 October 2011 already provided to her;

(d)   To prepare a draft recommendation in relation to the merits of communication No. 19/2008 for the twenty-second session of the Working Group;

(e)   To prepare a draft recommendation in relation to the admissibility of communication No. 25/2010, to be considered by the Working Group at its twenty-second session;

(f)   To prepare a draft recommendation on the admissibility and merits of communication No. 28/2010;

(g)   To transmit the State party's proposal in communication No. 24/2009 to engage in a friendly settlement to the author's counsel, with a one-month deadline to inform the Committee of his decision in that regard. The letter would also inform the author's counsel that such process would not result in the discontinuance of the case before the Committee unless the friendly settlement was successful and the author withdrew the case;

(h)   To continue its preliminary discussion of communication No. 30/2011 at its twenty-second session, in light of the pending response from the State party;

(i)   To postpone its discussion on the admissibility of communication No. 29/2011 to its twenty-second session, when the draft recommendation on admissibility would be available in all languages of the Working Group;

(j)   To reject the request submitted by Bulgaria to consider separately the admissibility and merits of communication No. 32/2011;

(k)   To appoint the case rapporteurs for communications Nos. 17/2008 (Ms. Bareiro-Bobadilla), 20/2008 (Ms. Šimonović) and 23/2009 (Ms. Hayashi) as follow-up rapporteurs for those communications, and to seek the appointment of co-rapporteurs for follow-up of those communications by the Committee during its fiftieth session;

(l)   To request the Secretariat to arrange a meeting with the Permanent Mission of the Philippines at the beginning of the Committee's fiftieth session to discuss follow-up to communication No. 18/2008;

(m)   To request the Secretariat to provide information to the Working Group at its twenty-second session on how other treaty bodies organize follow-up to communications, with a view to making a formal recommendation to the Committee's plenary to set up follow-up procedures;

(n) To reject the proposal to limit Working Group sessions to two per year (January/February and October), as it would impede the efficiency of the Committee's work, in that the latter would not be able to decide on individual communications for a period of seven to eight months; and, in light of the difficulties experienced with the servicing of the New York session of the Working Group, to propose that the Working Group hold three sessions in Geneva (three days in January/February, four days in May/June and three days in October);

(o) To discuss, at its twenty-second session, the possible registration of a communication submitted by an author against the United Kingdom of Great Britain and Northern Ireland on 24 February 2011 and 2 March 2011, which the Secretariat had dealt with by way of a standard letter;

(p) To write to the authors of a request for inquiry, received on 2 August 2011 and mistakenly processed by the Secretariat as an individual complaint, informing the authors that their request had been transmitted to the Committee for action under article 8 of the Optional Protocol.

13. Regarding its intersessional work and internal working methods, the Working Group decided the following:

(a) Registration, requests for interim measures and other important issues on registered communications should be agreed upon by at least three members of the Working Group;

(b) Specific requests such as extensions and splits in a registered case only require the agreement of the case rapporteur and the Chair of the Working Group, but should be transmitted for information to all Working Group members;

(c) Standard acknowledgments of receipt and transmittal of submissions in a registered case are to be dealt with by the Secretariat, copying the case rapporteur and the Chair of the Working Group;

(d) In case of doubt regarding a specific or complex issue, the Working Group should systematically be contacted;

(e) The Committee's focal point in the Petitions Unit should be consulted by other members of the Unit in the processing of all unregistered correspondence.

14. The Working Group submitted the following issues for the Committee's consideration and decision:

(a) One recommendation relating to the admissibility and merits of communication No. 22/2009;

(b) Two recommendations relating to the admissibility of communications Nos. 26/2010 and 27/2010;

(c) A proposal to hold all three sessions of the Working Group in Geneva, in light of the difficulties in servicing experienced in New York, or to maintain the current format of three sessions, including one session in New York, serviced by the Petitions Unit;

(d) The appointment of co-rapporteurs for follow-up of communications Nos. 17/2008 (rapporteur Ms. Bareiro-Bobadilla), 20/2008 (rapporteur Ms. Šimonović) and 23/2009 (rapporteur Ms. Hayashi);

(e)   The allocation of sufficient specialized staff in the Petitions Unit, in particular the P-4 post moved together with the Committee secretariat from New York to Geneva (Petitions Unit);

(f)   The improvement of the Committee's website with a view to reflecting all cases adopted by the Committee, including discontinuance decisions;

(g)   The inclusion of information on the Optional Protocol in the Committee's extranet page.

15.   The Working Group on Communications under the Optional Protocol to the Convention on the Elimination of All Forms of Discrimination against Women will hold its twenty-second session in Geneva from 7 to 10 February 2012.

Appendix

Agenda of the twenty-first session of the Working Group

1. Adoption of the agenda and organization of work.

2. Review of steps and activities undertaken since the last session.

3. New communications registered.

4. Discussion on cases ready for adoption.

5. Cases for discontinuance.

6. Update on communications.

7. Preliminary discussion on registered cases.

8. Update on follow-up on views.

9. Discussion on working methods, including the Committee's rules of procedure in relation to discontinuances, follow-up to views and duplication of international procedures ("forum shopping").

10. Update on outreach activities.

11. Adoption of the report of the Working Group on its twenty-first session.

Part Three
Report of the Committee on the Elimination of Discrimination against Women on its fifty-first session

13 February-2 March 2012

12-28161

Chapter I

Matters brought to the attention of the States parties to the Convention on the Elimination of All Forms of Discrimination against Women

Decisions

Decision 51/I

Taking note of the status of submissions information presented by the Secretariat (see annex I to part three of the present report), the Committee decided to request the following States with long overdue reports to submit all overdue reports on the dates specified and that, failing receipt of these reports, and as a last resort, the Committee will proceed with the consideration of the implementation of the Convention of those States parties in the absence of their reports: Antigua and Barbuda (combined fourth to seventh periodic reports due on 31 August 2014); Barbados (combined fifth to eighth periodic reports due on 2 March 2014); Saint Kitts and Nevis (combined fifth to eighth periodic reports due on 25 May 2014); Trinidad and Tobago (combined fourth to seventh periodic reports due on 11 February 2015). The Committee also requested the Secretariat to follow up as necessary with States parties with overdue reports.

Decision 51/II

With respect to request for inquiry No. 2011/1, the Committee decided to designate three Committee members to be in charge of the task force relating to this matter and to invite the State party concerned to submit observations within two months with regard to the information received by the Committee indicating grave or systematic violations of certain rights set forth in the Convention on the Elimination of All Forms of Discrimination against Women, in accordance with article 8, paragraph 2, of the Optional Protocol to the Convention. The Committee also decided to invite the State party concerned to cooperate with the Committee in the conduct of a possible inquiry and for that purpose to provide the designated members with any information that they or the State party may consider useful for ascertaining the facts relating to the matter, and indicate any other form of cooperation that the State party may wish to extend to the Committee and to its designated members with a view to facilitating the conduct of the inquiry, if warranted. The Committee also decided to request the State party concerned to agree to a possible country visit by the members designated by the Committee after consideration of the observations of the State party and in accordance with article 8, paragraph 2, of the Optional Protocol to the Convention, and rule 86 of the Rules of Procedure of the Committee. Lastly, the Committee decided to request the designated members to obtain and to examine in the most objective manner information relevant to the confidential inquiry that may be available from the State party or from other sources, and to report to the Committee at its fifty-second session in July 2012. Lastly, the Committee decided to request the Secretary-General to transmit the decision to the State party.

Decision 51/III

The Committee endorsed the decision of the Bureau to hold a thirtieth anniversary event at its fifty-second session in New York in July 2012 to commemorate the Committee's first session. The Committee also welcomed the generous invitation of the Government of Turkey to hold a two-day meeting in Istanbul in commemoration of the Committee's thirtieth anniversary in November 2012.

Decision 51/IV

The Committee confirmed Victoria Popescu and Yoko Hayashi as members of the joint working group of the Committee on the Elimination of Discrimination against Women and the Human Rights Committee.

Chapter II
Organizational and other matters

A. States parties to the Convention and to the Optional Protocol

1.   On 2 March 2012, the closing date of the fifty-first session of the Committee on the Elimination of Discrimination against Women, there were 187 States parties to the Convention on the Elimination of All Forms of Discrimination against Women, which was adopted by the General Assembly in its resolution 34/180 and opened for signature, ratification and accession in New York on 1 March 1980. In accordance with its article 27, the Convention entered into force on 3 September 1981. In addition, 65 Contracting States had accepted the amendment to article 20, paragraph 1, of the Convention, concerning the Committee's meeting time. A total of 125 States parties to the Convention are currently required to accept the amendment in order to bring it into force, in accordance with its provisions.

2.   As at the same date, there were 104 States parties to the Optional Protocol to the Convention, which was adopted by the General Assembly in its resolution 54/4 and opened for signature in New York on 10 December 1999. In accordance with its article 16, the Optional Protocol entered into force on 22 December 2000.

3.   Updated information on the status of the Convention, the amendment to the Convention and its Optional Protocol, including lists of States signatories and parties as well as the texts of declarations, reservations, objections and other relevant information can be found on the website of the United Nations Treaty Collection (http://treaties.un.org), maintained by the Treaty Section of the Office of Legal Affairs, which discharges the depositary functions of the Secretary-General.

B. Opening of the session

4.   The Committee held its fifty-first session at the United Nations Office at Geneva from 13 February to 2 March 2012. The Committee held 16 plenary meetings, and also held 14 meetings to discuss agenda items 5, 6, 7 and 8. A list of the documents before the Committee is contained in annex II to part three of the present report.

5.   The session was opened by the Chair of the Committee, Silvia Pimentel, on 13 February 2012. The Chief of the Women's Rights and Gender Section, Isha Dyfan, addressed the Committee at the opening of the session.

C. Adoption of the agenda

6.   The Committee adopted the provisional agenda (CEDAW/C/51/1) at its 1018th meeting.

D.   Report of the pre-session working group

7.   The report of the pre-session working group (CEDAW/PSWG/51/1), which met from 1 to 5 August 2011, was introduced by Victoria Popescu at the 1019th meeting.

E.   Organization of work

8.   On 13 February 2012, the Committee held a closed meeting with representatives of specialized agencies and United Nations funds and programmes, as well as other intergovernmental organizations, during which those bodies provided country-specific information as well as information on the efforts they had made to support the implementation of the Convention.

9.   On 13 and 20 February 2012, the Committee held informal public meetings with representatives of non-governmental organizations who provided information about the implementation of the Convention in the countries whose Governments were reporting to the Committee at its fifty-first session.

F.   Membership of the Committee

10.   All members except Indira Jaising attended the fifty-first session. Feride Acar and Nicole Ameline were absent for two days to attend the meeting of the Commission on the Status of Women. A list of members of the Committee, indicating the duration of their terms of office, is contained in annex V to part one of the present report.

Chapter III
Report of the Chair on activities undertaken between the fiftieth and fifty-first sessions of the Committee

11.   At the 1019th meeting, the Chair presented a report on the activities she had undertaken since the fiftieth session of the Committee.

Chapter IV

Consideration of reports submitted by States parties under article 18 of the Convention

12.   At its fifty-first session, the Committee considered the reports of seven States parties submitted under article 18 of the Convention: the combined third and fourth periodic reports of Algeria; the seventh periodic report of Brazil; the sixth periodic report of the Congo; the combined initial to fifth periodic reports of Grenada; the fifth periodic report of Jordan; the eighth periodic report of Norway; and the combined second to fifth periodic reports of Zimbabwe. Information on the status of submission and consideration of reports submitted by States parties under article 18 of the Convention can be obtained from the Treaty Body Database under "reporting status" at www.unhchr.ch/tbs/doc.nsf.

13.   The Committee prepared concluding observations on each of the reports considered. Those observations are available from the Official Document System of the United Nations (http://documents.un.org/) under the symbol numbers indicated below:

Algeria	(CEDAW/C/DZA/CO/3-4)
Brazil	(CEDAW/C/BRA/CO/7)
Congo	(CEDAW/C/COG/CO/6)
Grenada	(CEDAW/C/GRD/CO/1-5)
Jordan	(CEDAW/C/JOR/CO/5)
Norway	(CEDAW/C/NOR/CO/8)
Zimbabwe	(CEDAW/C/ZWE/CO/2-5)

Following the fifty-first session, observations on concluding observations of the Committee were submitted by Algeria and Norway.

Follow-up procedures relating to concluding observations

14.   The Committee adopted the report of the rapporteur on follow-up at its fifty-first session, and considered the follow-up reports from the following States parties:

Armenia	(CEDAW/C/ARM/CO/4/Rev.1/Add.1)
Belgium	(CEDAW/C/BEL/CO/6/Add.1)
Ecuador	(CEDAW/C/ECU/CO/7/Add.1)
Spain	(CEDAW/C/ESP/CO/6/Add.1)

The follow-up reports of the States parties and the Committee's replies are available on the Committee's web page hosted on the OHCHR website under "follow-up reports" at www2.ohchr.org/english/bodies/cedaw.

15.   The Committee also sent second reminders to the following States parties whose follow-up reports were overdue: Bhutan, Cameroon, Guinea-Bissau, Liberia and Timor-Leste.

12-28161

16.   The Committee sent a letter to El Salvador to schedule a meeting with a representative of that State party, which had not submitted its follow-up report despite two reminders sent by the Committee. The follow-up rapporteur met with the representative of El Salvador.

17.   The Committee extended further invitations to meet with representatives of Nigeria and the United Republic of Tanzania, which had not submitted their follow-up report despite two reminders sent by the Committee and had not replied to the letter sent at the fiftieth session to schedule a meeting with their representatives. The Committee did not receive any replies.

Chapter V

Activities carried out under the Optional Protocol to the Convention on the Elimination of All Forms of Discrimination against Women

18.   Article 12 of the Optional Protocol to the Convention on the Elimination of All Forms of Discrimination against Women provides that the Committee shall include in its annual report under article 21 of the Convention a summary of its activities under the Optional Protocol.

A.   Action taken by the Committee in respect of issues arising from article 2 of the Optional Protocol

19.   The Committee discussed activities under the Optional Protocol on 20, 24 and 28 February 2012.

20.   The Committee endorsed the report of the Working Group on Communications under the Optional Protocol on its twenty-second session (see annex III to part three of the present report).

21.   The Committee took action on communications Nos. 19/2008 (*Cecilia Kell v. Canada*), 25/2010 (*M.I. P.M. v. Canada*) and 28/2010 (*R.K.B. v. Turkey*) and adopted two views and one inadmissibility decision on those communications. The inadmissibility decision was adopted by consensus. One member expressed her intention to submit a dissenting individual opinion on the views in communication No. 19/2008 and one member expressed her intention to submit a concurring individual opinion on the views in communication No. 28/2010.

B.   Follow-up to views of the Committee on individual communications

22.   No specific follow-up action could be undertaken this session in relation to communication No. 18/2008 (*Karen Tayag Vertido v. the Philippines*), as the Permanent Mission of the Philippines did not respond to the Committee's request for a follow-up meeting, transmitted early in the session, as well as in the previous session. For the report of the Committee under the Optional Protocol on follow-up to views of the Committee on individual communications, see annex VII to part one of the present report.

C.   Action taken by the Committee in respect of issues arising from article 8 of the Optional Protocol

23.   Two additional requests for inquiries were received. These matters were not discussed by the Committee.

24.   With respect to request for inquiry No. 2011/1, the Committee decided to designate three Committee members to be in charge of the task force relating to this matter and to invite the State party concerned to submit observations within two months with regard to the information received by the Committee indicating grave or systematic violations of certain rights set forth in the Convention on the

Elimination of All Forms of Discrimination against Women, in accordance with article 8, paragraph 2, of the Optional Protocol to the Convention. The Committee also decided to invite the State party concerned to cooperate with the Committee in the conduct of a possible inquiry and for that purpose to provide the designated members with any information that they or the State party might consider useful for ascertaining the facts relating to the matter, and indicate any other form of cooperation that the State party might wish to extend to the Committee and to its designated members with a view to facilitating the conduct of the inquiry, if warranted. The Committee also decided to request the State party concerned to agree to a possible country visit by the members designated by the Committee after consideration of the observations of the State party and in accordance with article 8, paragraph 2, of the Optional Protocol of the Convention and rule 86 of the rules of procedure of the Committee. Lastly, the Committee decided to request the designated members to obtain and to examine in the most objective manner information relevant to the confidential inquiry that might be available from the State party or from other sources, and to report to the Committee at its fifty-second session in July 2012. Lastly, the Committee decided to request the Secretary-General to transmit the decision to the State party. A meeting was also held with members of the task force and representatives of the State party on 1 March 2012 to discuss areas of cooperation and to clarify procedures.

25.   The Committee was also briefed on the status of inquiry No. 2010/1 and was informed that the State party had indicated by letter dated 26 January 2012 that it intended to cooperate with the inquiry and had also requested detailed information on the visit, which would be treated as proposals subject to further approval. A letter in reply dated 21 February 2012 was transmitted to the Permanent Mission providing information relating to dates and duration, composition of the delegation, meetings and other relevant matters. The Committee further decided that if a reply were not received by 1 April, a reminder would be sent by the Secretariat.

26.   With respect to request for inquiry No. 2011/3, the Committee was informed that the task force had met to review the case and had concluded that there was insufficient information to take a decision on the matter and requested the Secretariat to draft a letter seeking additional information and clarification from the entity requesting the inquiry. The Committee endorsed the request by the task force. No update was provided with respect to request for inquiry No. 2011/2.

Chapter VI

Ways and means of expediting the work of the Committee

27. During its fifty-first session, the Committee considered agenda item 7, on ways and means of expediting the work of the Committee.

Action taken by the Committee under agenda item 7

Enhancing the Committee's working methods

28. The Working Group on Working Methods met during the session and approved a draft template to standardize the country briefing notes prepared by the country rapporteurs and also to facilitate their work in this regard. The draft template was distributed to the Committee for comments and it was decided that the issue required more discussion at the next session.

29. The Committee also undertook a preliminary review of the use of task forces and the overall impression of the Committee was that the task forces resulted in better time management during the constructive dialogues. Concerns were raised with respect to coverage of all relevant articles of the Convention and time allocated for questions. The Committee decided that the issue required more discussion at the next session.

30. The Committee also started to discuss the idea of permanent double chambers once a year as a way to address its increasing workload, especially with respect to requests for inquiries under article 8 of the Optional Protocol to the Convention, and the backlog in the consideration of State parties' reports. The Committee decided that the issue required more discussion at the next session.

31. Furthermore, the Committee was briefed on the Dublin II meeting and the recent informal consultation with States parties by Wan-Hea Lee and Paulo David of the Human Rights Treaties Division, including the issue of a master calendar for treaty body reporting. The Committee also met with the Chief of the Programme Support and Management Services, OHCHR, on travel-related issues.

Dates of future sessions of the Committee

32. In accordance with the calendar of conferences, the following dates were confirmed for the Committee's fifty-second and fifty-third sessions and related meetings:

(a) Twenty-third session of the Working Group on Communications under the Optional Protocol: 5-6 July 2012, New York;

(b) Fifty-second session: 9 to 27 July 2012, New York;

(c) Pre-session working group for the fifty-fourth session: 30 July to 3 August 2012, New York;

(d) Twenty-fourth session of the Working Group on Communications under the Optional Protocol: 25-28 September 2012, Geneva;

(e) Fifty-third session: 1 to 19 October 2012, Geneva;

(f)   Pre-session working group for the fifty-fifth session: 22 to 25 October 2012, Geneva.

Reports to be considered at future sessions of the Committee

33.   The Committee confirmed that it will consider the reports of the following States parties at its fifty-second and fifty-third sessions:

Fifty-second session

Bahamas
Bulgaria
Guyana
Indonesia
Jamaica
Mexico
New Zealand
Samoa

Fifty-third session

Central African Republic (in absence of a report)
Comoros
Chile
Equatorial Guinea
Serbia
Togo
Turkmenistan

Chapter VII
Implementation of article 21 of the Convention

34.   During the fifty-first session, the Committee considered agenda item 6, on the implementation of article 21 of the Convention.

Action taken by the Committee under agenda item 6

General recommendation on the economic consequences of marriage and its dissolution

35.   The working group met during the session and the Committee continued with the review of the draft general recommendation in plenary. The revised version will be circulated between sessions for additional comments, and the Committee will continue finalizing the draft general recommendation at its fifty-second session in July 2012.

General recommendation on women in conflict and post-conflict situations

36.   The working group met during the session but no discussions took place in plenary, although the Chair of the working group, Ms. Patten, briefed the Committee on recent developments. The working group, in conjunction with UN-Women and OHCHR, has been organizing various regional consultations to solicit input on issues relevant to the human rights of women in conflict and post-conflict situations. The regional consultations are scheduled to take place between March and May 2012 in Bangkok, Addis Ababa, Guatemala City and Istanbul.

Joint general recommendation on harmful practices

37.   The working group met twice with the United Nations Children's Fund during the session and drafting has commenced on several substantive topics under the general recommendation. There was no discussion in plenary on this issue.

General recommendation on access to justice

38.   The Chair of the working group, Ms. Pimentel, briefed the Committee on recent developments concerning the draft general recommendation and circulated a concept note, which the Committee decided it would need more time to review before its endorsing it. It was suggested that the concept note be revised and endorsed at the fifty-second session.

Working group on gender equality in the context of asylum, statelessness and natural disasters

39.   The working group met during the session with UNHCR to discuss the substantive issues under the general recommendation, and briefed the Committee in plenary. The working group will continue to work between sessions on a draft general recommendation.

Working group on rural women

40. There was no discussion in plenary on this issue. However, members of the working group exchanged information and documentation during the session and will continue to work between sessions on the subject.

Chapter VIII
Provisional agenda for the fifty-second session

41.   The Committee considered the draft provisional agenda for its fifty-second session on 2 March 2012 and approved the following provisional agenda for that session:

1.   Opening of the session.

2.   Adoption of the agenda and organization of work.

3.   Report of the Chair on activities undertaken between the fifty-first and fifty-second sessions of the Committee.

4.   Consideration of reports submitted by States parties under article 18 of the Convention on the Elimination of All Forms of Discrimination against Women.

5.   Follow-up to concluding observations of reports submitted by States parties under article 18 of the Convention on the Elimination of All Forms of Discrimination against Women.

6.   Implementation of articles 21 and 22 of the Convention on the Elimination of All Forms of Discrimination against Women.

7.   Ways and means of expediting the work of the Committee.

8.   Activities of the Committee under the Optional Protocol to the Convention on the Elimination of All Forms of Discrimination against Women.

9.   Provisional agenda for the fifty-third session of the Committee.

10.   Adoption of the report of the Committee on its fifty-second session.

Chapter IX
Adoption of the report

42. The Committee considered the draft report on its fifty-first session on 2 March 2012 and adopted it as orally revised during the discussion.

Annex I

Status of submission of overdue reports by States parties under article 18 of the Convention

Report of the Secretariat of the Committee

1.   Rule 49 of the rules of procedure of the Committee on the Elimination of Discrimination against Women provides that, at each session, the Secretary-General shall notify the Committee of the non-submission of any report that States parties are required to submit under article 18 of the Convention on the Elimination of All Forms of Discrimination against Women. In practice, this information is provided annually.

2.   Appendix I to the present report contains a list of 48 States parties whose reports are due or overdue and had not been submitted as at 31 December 2011. In some cases, the Committee has modified the date of submission calculated in accordance with article 18, paragraph 1, of the Convention, and this is reflected in the report.

3.   Appendix II to the present report contains a list of 13 States parties (out of the 48 States parties mentioned above) whose reports are five years or more overdue. Of these 13 States, four are scheduled to be considered in the absence of a report at upcoming sessions of the Committee based upon previous decisions of the Committee (Central African Republic, Saint Vincent and the Grenadines, Senegal and the Solomon Islands).

4.   The above overdue reports also include initial reports. Initial reports have not yet been received from the Cook Islands, Dominica, Kiribati, Micronesia, Monaco, San Marino, Sao Tome and Principe, Solomon Islands and Swaziland.

5.   It is further noted that from 1 January to 31 December 2011, 30 reports were received. During the same time period, the Committee considered 23 reports.

6.   In March 2011, the Secretariat transmitted reminders to the permanent missions of 34 States parties with overdue reports. Of the 34 States contacted, 11 submitted their overdue reports, including Afghanistan, Benin, Bosnia and Herzegovina, Cameroon, Cyprus, Dominican Republic, Hungary, Iraq, Qatar, Senegal and Tajikistan.

7.   Reminders were sent to the following remaining States with overdue reports in January 2012: Belize, Bolivia, Cook Islands, Croatia, Eritrea, Georgia, Ghana, Guinea, India, Ireland, Malaysia, Maldives, Mauritania, Mozambique, Namibia, Peru, Romania, Saint Lucia and Viet Nam.

8.   With respect to exceptional reports, the exceptional report of the Democratic Republic of the Congo was due on 16 November 2010. A reminder was transmitted to the Permanent Mission on 15 November 2011. The exceptional report of Guinea was due on 10 November 2009. Reminders were sent to the Permanent Mission on 10 October 2010 and 16 November 2011.

Appendix I

States parties whose reports are due and had not yet been submitted to the Committee as at 31 December 2011

State party	Date due
Antigua and Barbuda	
Combined fourth, fifth and sixth periodic reports	31 August 2010
Barbados	
Combined fifth, sixth and seventh periodic reports	3 September 2007
Eighth periodic report	3 September 2011
Belize	
Combined fifth and sixth periodic reports	15 June 2011
Bolivia	
Combined fifth and sixth periodic reports	8 July 2011
Brunei Darussalam	
Combined initial and second periodic reports	23 June 2011
Central African Republic	
Combined initial to fifth periodic reports	21 July 2008
	Scheduled to be considered in the absence of a report at the fifty-third session (decision taken at thirty-eighth session)
China	
Combined seventh and eighth periodic reports	3 September 2010
Cook Islands	
Initial report	10 September 2007
Second periodic report	10 September 2011
Croatia	
Combined fourth and fifth periodic reports	9 October 2009
Democratic People's Republic of Korea	
Second periodic report	27 March 2006

State party	Date due
Third periodic report	27 March 2010
Dominica	
Combined initial to seventh periodic reports	Considered in the absence of a report at the forty-third session
Eighth periodic report	31 December 2010
Eritrea	
Fourth periodic report	5 October 2008
Gabon	
Sixth and seventh combined reports	20 February 2008
Gambia	
Combined fourth and fifth periodic reports	16 May 2010
Georgia	
Combined fourth and fifth periodic reports	25 November 2011
Ghana	
Combined sixth and seventh periodic reports	1 February 2011
Guinea	
Combined seventh and eighth periodic reports	8 September 2011
India	
Combined fourth and fifth reports	8 August 2010
Ireland	
Sixth periodic report	22 January 2007
Seventh periodic report	22 January 2011
Kiribati	
Initial report	16 April 2005
Second periodic report	16 April 2009
Latvia	
Combined fourth and fifth periodic reports	14 May 2009
Malaysia	
Combined third and fourth periodic reports	4 August 2008

State party	Date due
Maldives	
Combined fourth and fifth periodic reports	31 July 2010
Mali	
Combined sixth and seventh periodic reports	10 October 2010
Marshall Islands	
Combined initial and second periodic reports	1 April 2011
Mauritania	
Combined second and third periodic reports	9 June 2010
Micronesia (Federated States of)	
Combined initial and second periodic reports	1 October 2009
Monaco	
Combined initial and second periodic reports	17 April 2010
Mozambique	
Combined third and fourth periodic reports	21 May 2010
Namibia	
Combined fourth and fifth periodic reports	31 December 2009
Nicaragua	
Combined seventh and eighth periodic reports	26 November 2010
Peru	
Combined seventh and eighth periodic reports	13 October 2011
Philippines	
Combined seventh and eighth periodic reports	4 September 2010
Poland	
Combined seventh and eighth periodic reports	3 September 2010
Romania	
Combined seventh and eighth periodic reports	6 February 2011
Saint Kitts and Nevis	
Fifth periodic report	25 May 2002
Sixth periodic report	25 May 2006

State party	Date due
Seventh periodic report	25 May 2010
Saint Lucia	
Seventh periodic report	7 November 2007
Eighth periodic report	7 November 2011
Saint Vincent and the Grenadines	
Combined fourth, fifth, sixth and seventh periodic reports	3 September 2006
Eighth periodic report	3 September 2010
	Scheduled for consideration in the absence of a report at the fifty-sixth session (decision taken at the forty-first session)
San Marino	
Initial report	9 January 2005
Second periodic report	9 January 2009
Sao Tome and Principe	
Initial report	3 July 2004
Second periodic report	3 July 2008
Senegal	
Combined third to seventh periodic reports	7 March 2010
	Scheduled for consideration in the absence of a report at the fifty-seventh session (decision taken at the forty-first session)
Solomon Islands	
Initial report	6 June 2003
Second periodic report	6 June 2007
Third periodic report	6 June 2011
	Scheduled for consideration in the absence of a report at the fifty-sixth session (decision taken at the forty-first session)

State party	Date due
Suriname	
Combined fourth and fifth periodic reports	31 March 2010
Swaziland	
Initial report	25 April 2005
Second periodic report	25 April 2009
Thailand	
Combined sixth and seventh periodic reports	8 September 2010
Trinidad and Tobago	
Fourth periodic report	11 February 2003
Fifth periodic report	11 February 2007
Sixth periodic report	11 February 2011
Venezuela (Bolivarian Republic of)	
Seventh periodic report	1 June 2008
Viet Nam	
Combined seventh and eighth periodic reports	19 March 2011

Appendix II

States parties whose reports were five years or more overdue as at 31 December 2011

State party
Antigua and Barbuda
Barbados
Central African Republic (decision taken to consider in absence of a report at thirty-eighth session)
Democratic People's Republic of Korea
Kiribati
Saint Kitts and Nevis
Saint Vincent and the Grenadines (decision taken to consider in absence of a report at the forty-first session)
San Marino
Sao Tome and Principe
Senegal (decision taken to consider in absence of a report at the forty-first session)
Solomon Islands (decision taken to consider in absence of a report at the forty-first session)
Swaziland
Trinidad and Tobago

12-28161

Appendix III

Tentative schedule of consideration of the implementation of the Convention by States parties at upcoming sessions of the Committee on the Elimination of Discrimination against Women

Fifty-second session (9 to 27 July 2012)

- Bahamas
- Bulgaria
- Guyana
- Indonesia
- Jamaica
- Mexico
- New Zealand
- Samoa

Fifty-third session (1 to 19 October 2012)

- Central African Republic (in the absence of a report)
- Chile
- Comoros
- Equatorial Guinea
- Serbia
- Togo
- Turkmenistan

Fifty-fourth session (February 2013)

- Angola
- Austria
- Cyprus
- Greece
- Hungary
- Pakistan
- Solomon Islands (in the absence of a report)
- The former Yugoslav Republic of Macedonia

Fifty-fifth session (July 2013)

- Afghanistan
- Bosnia and Herzegovina
- Cape Verde
- Cuba
- Democratic Republic of the Congo
- Dominican Republic
- United Kingdom

Fifty-sixth session (October 2013)

- Andorra
- Benin
- Cambodia
- Colombia
- Republic of Moldova
- Saint Vincent and the Grenadines (in the absence of a report)
- Seychelles
- Tajikistan

Annex II

Documents before the Committee at its fifty-first session

Document number	Title or description
CEDAW/C/51/1	Provisional agenda and schedule of dialogues
CEDAW/C/51/2	Report of the United Nations Educational, Scientific and Cultural Organization
CEDAW/C/51/3	Report of the International Labour Organization
Reports of States parties	
CEDAW/C/DZA/3-4	Combined third and fourth periodic reports of Algeria
CEDAW/C/BRA/7	Seventh periodic report of Brazil
CEDAW/C/COG/6	Sixth periodic report of the Congo
CEDAW/C/GRD/1-5	Combined initial to fifth periodic reports of Grenada
CEDAW/C/JOR/5	Fifth periodic report of Jordan
CEDAW/C/NOR/8	Eighth periodic report of Norway
CEDAW/C/ZWE/2-5	Combined second to fifth periodic reports of Zimbabwe

Annex III

Report of the Working Group on Communications under the Optional Protocol to the Convention on the Elimination of All Forms of Discrimination against Women on its twenty-second session

1.   The Working Group on Communications under the Optional Protocol to the Convention on the Elimination of All Forms of Discrimination against Women held its twenty-second session from 7 to 10 February 2012. All members attended the session. Mr. Bruun was absent for the last day of the meeting.

2.   At the beginning of the session, the Working Group adopted its agenda as set out in the appendix to the present report.

3.   At its twenty-second session, the Working Group reviewed the update on new correspondence received by the Secretariat since its last session. The Working Group had before it a table of correspondence received or processed between 3 August and 5 December 2011, as well as a table dividing that correspondence into five categories, as requested by the Working Group at its twentieth session. It also noted that between sessions, two new communications had been registered, one of which included a request for interim measures of protection.

4.   The Working Group reviewed unregistered correspondence and decided that, in two cases, the authors should be contacted again with a deadline for response by the end of the Working Group's session to confirm their wish to have their communication registered. On 8 February 2012, both authors confirmed their interest in having their communication registered. One communication concerns the impossibility of transmission of citizenship and the other one relates to domestic violence and child custody issues.

5.   The Working Group requested the Secretariat to systematically consult it in cases of domestic violence and in cases where the Secretariat is in doubt before replying to the author.

6.   During its session, the Working Group reviewed the status of pending registered communications and had a discussion on each of them.

7.   The Working Group discussed two draft recommendations on admissibility in relation to communications Nos. 25/2010 and 29/2011 and two draft recommendations on the admissibility and merits of communications Nos. 19/2008 and 28/2010.

8.   The Working Group had a preliminary discussion on communication No. 31/2011.

9.   The Working Group discussed follow-up with regard to communication No. 18/2008 and took note of information with regard to communication No. 20/2008.

10.   The Chair of the Working Group briefed her colleagues on the expert consultations on petitions held on 29 October 2011 in Geneva.

11.   Ms. Patten and Mr. Bruun briefed their colleagues on a meeting they had during the session with staff members of the International Labour Organization

dealing with ILO Convention 100 on Equal Remuneration and ILO Convention 111 on Discrimination (Employment and Occupation), during which they discussed possibilities of future cooperation.

12. The Working Group expressed its appreciation for the establishment of the Optional Protocol extranet, which will facilitate the preparation of the cases.

Actions taken

13. At its twenty-second session, the Working Group decided:

(a) To adopt a recommendation in relation to the admissibility of communication No. 25/2010;

(b) To adopt recommendations in relation to the admissibility and the merits of communications Nos. 19/2008 (the Committee took a decision on the admissibility on 15 October 2010) and 28/2010;

(c) To postpone the adoption of a recommendation in relation to the admissibility of communication No. 29/2011 to the Working Group's twenty-third session;

(d) To prepare a draft recommendation for the twenty-third session on communication No. 32/2011;

(e) To prepare a draft recommendation, provided that comments by the author are received in time, for the twenty-third session on communication No. 31/2011;

(f) To register two new cases, one against Denmark and one against the United Kingdom, as communications Nos. 37/2012 and 38/2012, respectively;

(g) To request the Secretariat to systematically consult the Working Group on correspondence related to issues of domestic violence and in cases where the Secretariat is in doubt;

(h) To appoint the case rapporteurs for new communications Nos. 35/2011 (Ms. Patten), 36/2012 (Mr. Bruun), 37/2012 (Ms. Šimonović) and 38/2012 (Ms. Hayashi);

(i) To request that additional letters be sent in two pieces of unregistered correspondence, one relating to the question of exhaustion of domestic remedies and the other one with regard to the State party against which the complaint was directed;

(j) To postpone the preliminary discussion of communication No. 30/2011 to its twenty-third session, as no new information has been received;

(k) To request the Secretariat to organize a meeting with the Philippines for the follow-up rapporteurs, Ms. Patten and Ms. Neubauer, with regard to communication No. 18/2008;

(l) To request the Secretariat to include information and a table with an overview of information on follow-up on the Optional Protocol extranet;

(m) To ask the Secretariat to provide the Working Group at its next session with information on the modalities of follow-up of other treaty bodies with communications procedures, if available.

14. Regarding its intersessional work and internal working methods, the Working Group decided the following:

(a) To start considering modalities for follow-up to views;

(b) To amend and clarify the categories of unregistered correspondence as provided for in the note by the Secretariat.

15. The Working Group submitted the following issues for the Committee's consideration and decision:

(a) One recommendation relating to the admissibility and the merits of communication No. 19/2008 (admissibility decision of 15 October 2010);

(b) One recommendation relating to the admissibility of communication No. 25/2010;

(c) One recommendation relating to the admissibility and the merits of communication No. 28/2010;

(d) The allocation of sufficient specialized staff in the Petitions Unit, in particular the P-4 post moved together with the Committee secretariat from New York to Geneva (Petitions Unit).

16. The Working Group on Communications under the Optional Protocol to the Convention on the Elimination of All Forms of Discrimination against Women will hold its twenty-third session in New York on 5 and 6 July 2012.

12-28161 (E)   040512   310512

Please recycle

12-28161